SITTING IN: ROCK GUITAR
Backing Tracks and Improv Lessons

JARED MEEKER

In addition to MP3 demonstration and backing tracks, the companion DVD includes Alfred's exclusive TNT 2 software, which allows users to customize the audio tracks in this book for practice. Use it to slow down tracks, isolate and loop parts, and change tempos and keys.

To install, insert the DVD into the disc drive of your computer.

Windows
Double-click on **My Computer**, right-click on the DVD drive icon, and select **Explore**. Open the **TnT2** folder, then the **Windows** folder, and double-click on the installer file.

Macintosh
Double-click on the DVD icon on your desktop. Open the **TnT2** folder, then the **Mac** folder, and double-click on the installer file.

TNT 2 SYSTEM REQUIREMENTS

Windows
XP, Vista, 7, 8
QuickTime 7.6.7 or higher
1.8 GHz processor or faster
3.9 GB hard drive space
2 GB RAM minimum
DVD drive for installation
Speakers or headphones
Internet access for updates

Macintosh
OS 10.4 and higher (Intel only)
QuickTime 7.6.7 or higher
3.9 GB hard drive space
2 GB RAM minimum
DVD drive for installation
Speakers or headphones
Internet access for updates

Alfred Music
P.O. Box 10003
Van Nuys, CA 91410-0003
alfred.com

ISBN-10: 1-4706-2367-6 (Book & DVD-ROM)
ISBN-13: 978-1-4706-2367-8 (Book & DVD-ROM)

Audio recorded by Jared Meeker at Spiderfingers Studios, Valencia, CA.
Blake Colie (drums), Tristan Garcia (bass), Jamie Hinckson (keyboards), Tristan Garcia (trombone), Eddie Felix (alto saxophone)

Cover Photos
Keyboardist: Dale Berman • Guitarist: © iStockphoto / Jan Kowalski • Bassist: © iStockphoto / Rapid Eye Media
Drummer: © iStockphoto / Aleksandar Georgiev
Author photo: Katrine Lieberkind

 Alfred Cares. Contents printed on environmentally responsible paper.

CONTENTS

SONGS BY CATEGORY

CLASSIC ROCK

BLUES-ROCK

HARD ROCK

FUNK ROCK

COUNTRY ROCK

ALTERNATIVE ROCK

HEAVY METAL

ABOUT THE AUTHOR

 PHOTO © JASON HERRICK

Guitarist, composer, producer, educator, and author Jared Meeker has performed throughout the world playing blues, rock, Latin, reggae, metal, R&B, funk, hip-hop, and soul. Jared graduated from California Institute of the Arts and has taught at USC, UCLA, Seattle Pacific University, SUNY, Los Angeles Music Academy, and the National Guitar Workshop. Jared has worked with Salvador Santana (son of Carlos Santana), Nate Dogg, Snoop Dogg, Myka 9, N.A.S.A./Squeak E. Clean, Karen O, and Hollie Cook (daughter of Paul Cook from the Sex Pistols).

Along with releasing several albums of original music, Jared's compositions have appeared in award-winning films and on various programs on MTV, Showtime, NBC, VH1, CBS, and TNT. Jared has appeared in *Premier Guitar, Guitar Player,* and *Guitar World,* and is sponsored and endorsed by Line 6, Propellerhead software, Mesa Boogie amplifiers, Pigtronix effects, and Spalt Instruments. To learn more, visit jaredmeeker.com.

Acknowledgments

I am grateful for the opportunity to present these musical ideas to you. A big thanks goes out to my family for their love and support, specifically to my wife, Shelby; my kids, Miles and Liv; my mother and father, Maryanne and John; my mother- and father-in-law, Al and Laurie; and my extended family. Massive respect goes to the teachers, artists, students, mentors, and colleagues who have influenced my life. I'd also like to thank Ron Manus, Link Harnsberger, Nat Gunod, Donny Trieu, Matt Humphrey, and all the great Alfred Music employees for their hard work, friendship, and support in helping me bring this book to life.

About the DVD-ROM

In addition to TNT 2 software (with its own embedded audio tracks), MP3s are also included on the accompanying DVD-ROM. The symbol shown to the left appears next to every song in the book and is used to identify the TNT 2 tracks and MP3s on the DVD ("Track 1," "Track 2," "Track 3," etc.). Track 1 will help you get your guitar in tune.

To access the MP3s on the DVD, insert the DVD into the disc drive of your computer. In Windows, double-click on My Computer, then right-click on the DVD icon labeled "Sitting In – Rock Guitar" and select Explore to view the "MP3s" folder and copy it to your hard drive. For Mac, double-click on the DVD icon on your desktop labeled "Sitting In – Rock Guitar" to view the "MP3s" folder and copy it to your hard drive.

INTRODUCTION

The real life of rock music is in the club—backstage, out front, and onstage—where, night after night, artists put blood, sweat, and tears into refining their sound and style. For this very reason and as a tribute, each song in this book is named after a famous nightclub or venue. Over the course of 15 songs, we highlight 15 of the most historic and legendary rock music venues.

This book focuses on six rock genres, but keep in mind that the lines between genres are often blurred. When some of the legendary clubs were in their heyday, they booked wildly different acts on the same night, and that allowed (and perhaps encouraged) new, tradition-defying sounds to emerge. These days, bands are often booked at shows together because they have similar sounds.

Music Theory Background

While not essential, an understanding of basic music theory—such as the major scale, triads, and 7th chords—will make this book easier to use. This book also assumes you can read tablature (TAB) and/or standard music notation, are familiar with key signatures and time signatures, and have been playing chords, songs, and licks with pentatonic scales. Familiarity with the use of Roman numerals for understanding chord progressions will also help.

In this book, styles are grouped by sonic similarities. Take, for example, Led Zeppelin and Soundgarden, which are two groups separated by 20 years historically but share many of the same traits sonically. If Led Zeppelin had started in Seattle in the 1990s, they might have shared the bill with Soundgarden at Seattle's famed Crocodile Cafe. The key to being able to "sit in" with many bands as an experienced rock guitarist is the ability to accent the unique flavors of many different rock styles. We hope to provide you with tons of inspiration for writing, playing, and rocking out with others. Enjoy!

HOW TO USE THIS BOOK

Start with the Introduction to Rock Harmony. This will provide insight on the music theory behind rock music and offer a practical way to attain good fretboard knowledge as you improvise over the songs in this book. It will also give you ideas for creating variations of the rock licks presented here, which will enable you to follow the chord changes in a song.

This book is built around 15 compositions, which are presented in ascending *chromatic* (by *half step*, or one fret) order, starting with A Major, and increase in *tempo* (speed), starting at 60 *BPM* (beats per minute) and ending at 200 BPM. When you're done, you will have experience with all 12 key centers and a vast spectrum of feels. Plus, all 15 songs have been recorded by a professional live band that features drums, bass, keyboards, and guitar.

After each composition is a **Roadmap**, which shows how the sections of the tune are organized. After the Roadmap is the **Overview**, which provides insight into the song and a brief discussion of the style and feel. **Listening Suggestions** accompany each composition with examples of rock greats that play in similar feels to give you sources for vocal melodies, riffs, and licks. The **Licks** section provides ideas for soloing and is also designed to develop your musicianship as it focuses on four areas: timing, playing in different keys, fretboard knowledge, and harmony.

Timing

Timing is a critical part of good musicianship. Imagine a drummer playing fills at 90 BPM. If the tempo was changed to 120 BPM, the drummer would need to reconsider his or her phrasing ideas. Similarly, a guitarist should practice playing and improvising various tempos and feels. This book contains 15 backing tracks at 15 different tempos that represent the entire spectrum of feels and tempos that are expected of rock guitarists.

Playing in Different Keys

Practicing in many keys will strengthen your understanding of the fretboard, ear training, and note relationships. The TNT software that accompanies this book will allow you to transpose any of the songs into other keys. This is a wonderful way to go even deeper with your studies.

Fretboard Knowledge

Another benefit to working through this book is it will increase your fretboard knowledge, enabling you to solo in all positions on the neck. The Licks sections divide the neck into five positions and provides a lick or two for each position. Understanding these five shapes will allow you to use the entire fretboard, giving you more range and musical expression.

Harmony

Another part of your musicianship to focus on is harmony. The 15 songs introduce many unique modal sounds; mastering rhythm playing and soloing in these modes will unlock your creativity and prepare you for a variety of musical situations.

Soloing

The Soloing section covers concepts and scales for improvising on the form. It includes lessons on playing over changes and ideas for getting into the style and feel of the tune.

At the end of the book is an Appendix that includes the scales used throughout the book.

WORKING WITH THE PLAY-ALONG TRACKS

The included DVD-ROM features three sets of play-along options for optimizing your practice sessions. You get the following:

- An MP3 recording of each tune with a full band, including guitar, keyboards, bass, and drums
- An MP3 recording of each tune with the band, minus the guitar
- TNT 2 software, which allows you to isolate and loop sections, choose which instruments you want in the mix, and even to change tempos and keys

In each case, you get multiple choruses of each song played by a top-notch professional rock band. Each song contains a statement of the written main melody (or *head)*, followed by a guitar solo and keyboard solo before the head is restated. The length of each of these portions is laid out in the Roadmap that follows each song in the book.

The first set of MP3s (with guitar) acts as a demonstration, with the guitar playing a few straightforward soloing and comping ideas to exemplify how you can play over these tracks.

The second set of MP3s (without guitar) contains the backing tracks. Here, you play the head. A keyboard solo follows to provide some inspiring soloing ideas, providing you with more opportunity to comp. Then, there is space for you to practice soloing.

The TNT 2 software offers a host of other options. The transposition option allows you to try a song out in different keys, while the tempo-changing option can slow down a song to help with learning it or, as you are more advanced, speed it up to challenge yourself. You can also choose which instruments are in the mix and can *loop* (continuously repeat) specific sections by selecting a phrase in the software. There are many options for how you can play and interact with this book! The main goal is to have fun and keep your practice, jamming, and ideas creative and fresh. Enjoy!

SCALE THEORY

A *scale* is an arrangement of notes in a specific order of *whole steps* (two frets) and *half steps* (one fret). The major scale is made up of seven notes which, when played in sequence, make the familiar melody: do–re–mi–fa–sol–la–ti–(do). The scale is constructed by starting on any note and following this pattern of whole steps and half steps: W–W–H–W–W–W–H.

Major Scale

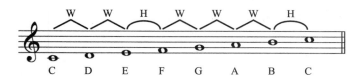

$\overset{W}{\wedge}$	= Whole step
$\overset{H}{\frown}$	= Half step

There are 12 notes in music, and a major scale can be built from any of the 12 notes. In order to maintain the pattern of steps that make up a major scale, every scale starting on any of the notes has its own combination of flats or sharps (except for C Major, which is comprised of natural notes). The name of the note that the scale starts from is called the *tonic* (although rock musicians often call it the *root,* so in this book, we'll use that term). To the right are all 12 major scales. Notice every note in a scale (the *scale degrees*) is numbered.

Root 1	2	3	4	5	6	7	8
A	B	C#	D	E	F#	G#	A
B♭	C	D	E♭	F	G	A	B♭
B	C#	D#	E	F#	G#	A#	B
C	D	E	F	G	A	B	C
D♭	E♭	F	G♭	A♭	B♭	C	D♭
D	E	F#	G	A	B	C#	D
E	F#	G#	A	B	C#	D#	E
F	G	A	B♭	C	D	E	F
F#	G#	A#	B	C#	D#	E#	F#
G	A	B	C	D	E	F#	G
A♭	B♭	C	D♭	E♭	F	G	A♭

The major scale is the standard to which all other scales are related. As you saw above, the individual notes (called *scale degrees*) of the major scale are numbered 1–8, and other scales are often described as alterations of these degrees. The scales (with formulas) used in this book are to the right:

Major Scale (Ionian):	1	2	3	4	5	6	7	8
Mixolydian:	1	2	3	4	5	6	♭7	8
Dominant 9 Pentatonic:	1	2	3	5	♭7	8		
Major Blues Scale:	1	2	♭3	3	5	6	8	
Dominant ♭9 Pentatonic:	1	♭2	3	5	♭7	8		
Dorian:	1	2	♭3	4	5	6	♭7	8
Aeolian:	1	2	♭3	4	5	♭6	♭7	8
Phrygian:	1	♭2	♭3	4	5	♭6	♭7	8

INTRO TO ROCK HARMONY

There are several chord concepts presented in this book, and some are simple while others are more complex. Let's take a look at each of them.

Diatonic Harmony: Diatonic means "within a key," so diatonic harmony refers to the chords that are created when the notes of a key are combined. Generally, this refers to two different kinds of keys: major and minor.

Roman Numeral System: Throughout this book, chords are discussed using Roman numerals. For example, a chord built on the 5th scale degree is called V. Uppercase numerals are used for major chords; lowercase numerals are used for minor and diminished chords. For diminished chords, the symbol ° is used with the Roman numeral, and for augmented chords, the symbol + is used.

The diatonic harmony of any major key is: I–ii–iii–IV–V–vi–vii°. In the key of C, that would be: C Major–D Minor–E Minor–F Major–G Major–A Minor–B Diminished.

Relative Minor: The relative minor key is a minor key built on the sixth degree of a major scale. Thus, it has the same notes and chords as the major key but in a different order with the emphasis placed on a different note as the root. For example, the relative minor of C Major is A Minor, so the new order of the chords is vi–vii°–I–ii–iii–IV–V, which is A Minor–B Diminished–C Major–D Minor–E Minor–F Major–G Major.

Modal Harmony: The concept of relative minor and relative major sharing the same notes but starting on different roots can be applied to all seven notes of the major scale. Here are the seven modes in the key of C. Each reordering of a major scale is called a mode. Below are the modes of the C Major scale:

C *Ionian**:	C–D–E–F–G–A–B–C	I–ii–iii–IV–V–vi–vii°–I
D *Dorian*:	D–E–F–G–A–B–C–D	ii–iii–IV–V–vi–vii°–I–ii
E *Phrygian*:	E–F–G–A–B–C–D–E	iii–IV–V–vi–vii°–I–ii–iii
F *Lydian*:	F–G–A–B–C–D–E–F	IV–V–vi–vii°–I–ii–iii–IV
G *Mixolydian*:	G–A–B–C–D–E–F–G	V–vi–vii°–I–ii–iii–IV–V
A *Aeolian***:	A–B–C–D–E–F–G–A	vi–vii°–I–ii–iii–IV–V–vi
B *Locrian*:	B–C–D–E–F–G–A–B	vii°–I–ii–iii–IV–V–vi– vii°

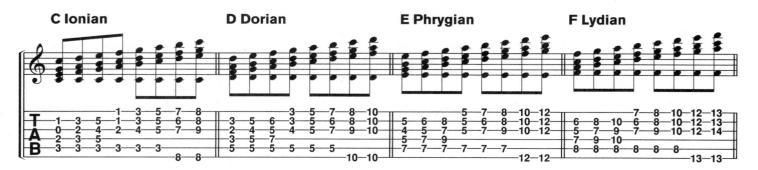

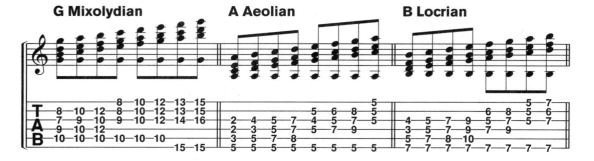

* Ionian is the same as the major scale.
** Also called the *natural minor scale*.

Tonic-Based Roman Numeral System

Throughout this book we use a *tonic-based Roman numeral system,* so the common resolution chord or tonic of the song is called the I, or i, instead of relating it to a *parent key* (the major key from which the mode is derived). For example, in D Dorian, the Dmin chord is i, even though it is ii in the parent key (C Major). This helps ground the relationship of the chords to the tonic, and will help us relate the mode, or scale, to its parallel major. Take a look below at the Roman numerals for all the modes in C, along with their correlating chord symbols which are shown to the right:

C Major or Ionian   I–ii–iii–IV–V–vi–vii°– I   C–Dmin–Emin–F–G–Amin–Bdim–C
C Dorian   i–ii–♭III–IV–v–vi°–♭VII–i   Cmin–Dmin–E♭–Fmaj–Gmin–Adim–B♭–Cmin
C Phrygian   i–♭II–♭III–iv–v°–♭IV–♭vii–i   Cmin–D♭–E♭–Fmin–Gdim–A♭–B♭min–Cmin
C Lydian   I–II–iii–♯iv–V–vi–vii–I   C–D–Emin–F♯dim–G–Amin–Bmin–C
C Mixolydian   I–ii–iii°–IV–v–vi–♭VII–I   C–Dmin–Edim–F–Gmin–Amin–B♭–C
C Aeolian   i–ii°–♭III–iv–v–♭IV–♭VII–i   Cmin–Ddim–E♭–F–Gmi–A♭–B♭–Cmin
C Locrian   i°–♭II–♭iii–iv–♭V–♭IV–♭vi–i°   Cdim–D♭–E♭min–Fmin–G♭–A♭–B♭min–Cdim

While we're at it, let's explore two additional modes that aren't from the major scale family: the *harmonic minor scale* (natural minor scale with a ♯7) and *Phrygian Dominant scale* (Phrygian with a ♯3, which is the fifth mode of harmonic minor).

C Harmonic Minor   i–ii°–♭III+–iv–V–♭IV–vii°–i   Cmin–Ddim–E♭aug–Fmin–G–A♭–Bdim–Cmin
C Phrygian Dominant   I–♭II–iii°–iv–v°–♭IV+–♭vi–I   C–D♭–Edim–Fmin–Gdim–A♭aug–B♭min–C

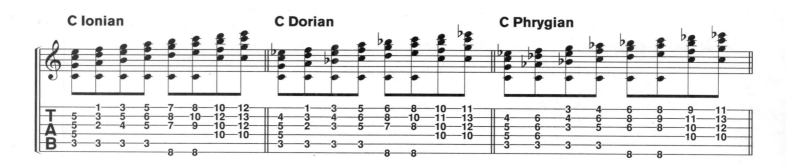

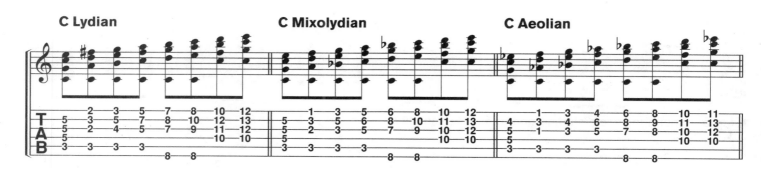

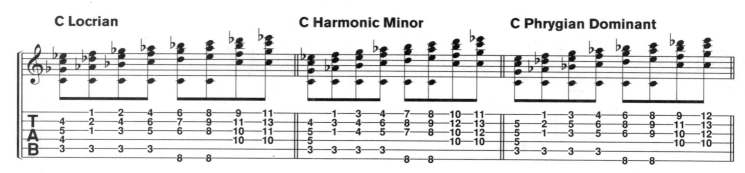

CHANGING KEYS AND MAKING THE CHANGES

It's common for a song to change keys. For instance, let's look at a standard 12-bar blues.

A7–A7–A7–A7–D7–D7–A7–A7–E7–D7–A7–E7

While there are often only three chords in a standard blues progression, each one is a dominant 7th chord (1–3–5–♭7), so each chord is a new key because, in diatonic harmony, dominant 7th chords are found on the V chord of the key. With the tonic-based Roman numeral system, the 12-bar blues can be analyzed like this:

I7–I7–I7–I7–IV7–I7–I7–I7–V7–IV7–I7–V7

Knowing the key(s) and scale(s) for a song is important to being able to improvise a solo. Following is an exercise that will help you learn to how to *make the changes* (in a solo, changing the notes you play to work over the chord being played) in a 12-bar blues in A.

Step 1: Ascend the A Major Blues scale starting on the root of each chord. In relation to the A Major scale, the A Major Blues scale formula is 1–2–♭3–3–5–6. Below are the three scales for each chord. Practice them in the context of the blues progression above. Once you get these specific fingerings down, play them elsewhere on the neck and in other octaves with new fingerings.

Step 2: Descend the scale starting on the root of each chord. Try reading the scales above from right to left.

Step 3: Ascend the scale starting on the 3rd of each chord.

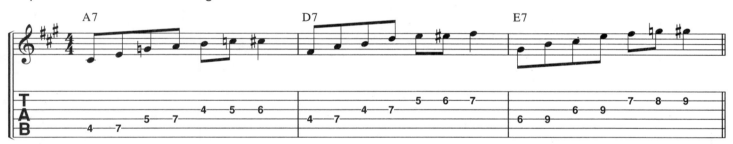

Step 4: Descend the scale starting on the 3rd.

Step 5: Ascend the scale starting on the 5th of each chord.

Step 6: Descend the scale starting on the 5th.

Isolating each chord as its own tonality is an important technique for targeting the harmonies in your melodies and lead lines. This is especially important when a progression moves out of key. Learn to analyze the harmony in songs to understand when they are diatonic, modal, or have chords that move out of key. This will help you go through chords progression in a natural, musical way.

Varying a Lick for the Chord Changes in the Same Position

Each song in this book includes at least five licks to serve as inspiration for soloing. Think of these as potential *themes* (main melody). Practice them repeatedly but also find ways to vary each to make the chord changes. Let's work on *transposing* (changing the key) of a lick. The first method for doing this is to stay in the same general fretboard position, then alter some of the notes to target the notes of the new chord. Let's first start with the theme. Here's a lick for the I chord in the key of A.

There are several ways to modify this lick to play over the IV chord (D7). Here, we will use D Dominant Pentatonic* and a bit of D Mixolydian at the end. Notice, it is essentially the same lick moved over to the next string set with a few alterations.

For the V (E7) and IV (D7) chords in bars 9–10, we can alter the original lick by staying in the same general register but using notes of E Dominant and then D Dominant Pentatonic. There are two themes to explore in the lick: the quarter-note hits and the 16th-note melody. Let's explore elaborating on the latter.

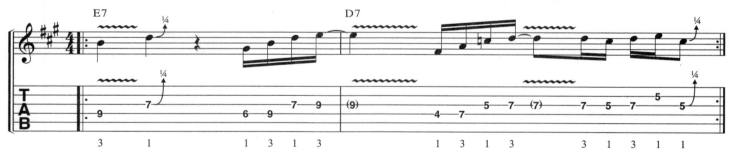

Varying a Lick for the Chord Changes by Moving Up and Down the Neck

Let's check out some ideas for transposing licks to follow the harmony of the blues progression through moving up or down the neck. Below is a lick using the F Minor Blues scale. You could use this over the entire blues progression, but it certainly sounds best on the I chord, F9.

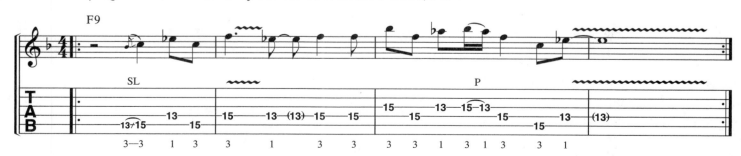

* Scale diagrams are available in the Appendix, pages 78–80. They are explained on page 13.

While still on the I chord (F9), let's move the lick back three frets. This turns it into a major blues shape, creating a distinctly major sound. Mixing up major and minor within the blues gives us a rise-and-fall or happy-and-sad effect.

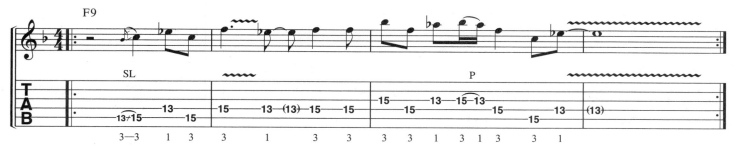

Now let's move the lick to the IV chord (B♭9). Take the original lick up two frets and you have a strong new sound as it becomes a major blues shape over the IV chord.

Next let's try that strategy for the V chord (C9). You could move the original lick up four frets or, in this case, down eight to create a major blues scale shape for C9.

The last tonality to go over is the minor sound over the V chord. This works great if you stay in the tonic minor blues for the whole progression or just accent the V with its own minor sound. To modify the original lick, you can slide it up seven frets (or down five) to create a minor blues scale shape over the V chord.

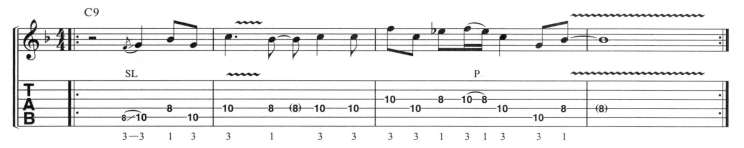

Finally let's talk about the shortening or lengthening of licks. Many of the licks in this book are four bars long, but sometimes the chord you'd like to play over is only two bars long—sometimes only one. In such cases, you can truncate the lick: cut it in half, or less, and just use that fragment transposed or otherwise varied to fit the chord progression. This will give you the option of using the first or last two bars of the lick as your theme. Experiment and have fun! The licks provided here are intended as inspiration, so don't let them limit you in any way.

SAY WHA?
(Classic Rock in A)

Track 2 (Full Mix)
Track 2A (Minus Guitar Lead)

Roadmap

Eight total choruses: head, guitar solo, keyboard solo (two choruses), guitar solo (three choruses), head.

Overview

This piece is named after the nightclub Cafe Wha? Located in the Greenwich Village neighborhood of New York City, Cafe Wha? was an epicenter of early rock culture. Bob Dylan, Jimi Hendrix, Bruce Springsteen, and the Velvet Underground all got their start playing and hanging out there.

This song is in the classic rock style but, if played with the right guitar effects, it could also be a psychedelic rock tune. When playing the melody, use a clean sound with a phaser, a touch of delay, and reverb for an atmospheric vibe. When soloing, experiment with adding overdrive, distortion, or fuzz for a soaring lead tone.

Since this piece is in a slow 16th-note groove, there is more room to be rhythmically off, as the distance between beats is greater here than at faster tempos. Be sure to play with emotion and stay *in the pocket* (locked into the groove). Lastly, this is a moody piece, so turn up, tap in, and let go.

- General form: I | IV | I | IV | I | IV | iii IV V | I

- Key: A

- ♩ = 60

Listening Suggestions

Stevie Ray Vaughan: "Lenny"
This classic tune by Stevie Ray Vaughan is very much inspired by the songwriting style of Jimi Hendrix on tunes like "Angel" and "Little Wing." Vaughan's song was written for, and named after, his wife, Lenora. Stevie also had a guitar named Lenny.

Red Hot Chili Peppers: "Under the Bridge"
John Frusciante, guitarist for the Red Hot Chili Peppers, played sweet riffs and chord patterns on this hit. Check out the dynamic range of this track: first, the guitar and vocals are alone, then bass and drums join in, and then there's a big build-up to the backup vocals.

Soloing

There are two basic scales at work in this tune: the A Major scale and the A Major Blues scale. For each of these scales, we'll focus on the five basic shapes below. Experiment with these shapes, and invent your own licks with the ideas from this chapter.

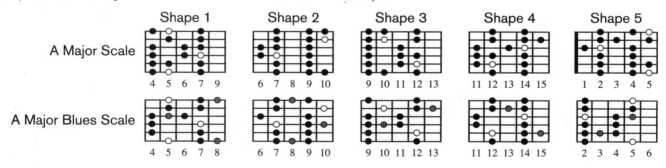

Scale Diagrams

This book makes extensive use of *scale diagrams.* To the right is an example of how to read a scale diagram.

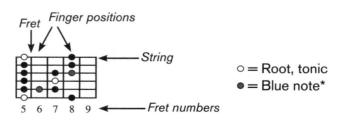

○ = Root, tonic
● = Blue note*

* In this context, a *blue note* is a *chromatic* tone (sharp or flat) added between two notes of a standard pentatonic scale to give it a bluesy edge.

Licks

The licks in this book are based on five basic scale shapes. Each shape is on a different part of the guitar fretboard. If you are not familiar with these scales, check out the Appendix on page 72.

Lick for Shape 1

All the 16th-note subdivisions may make this first lick look fast, but keep in mind the slow tempo. You just have to *lay back in the pocket* (focus on the musical pulse) to make the melodies groove. Also make sure your vibrato is nice, slow, and in time. Remember, you can transpose and modify this lick to make it work over any chord in the progression.

A Major Scale
Shape 1

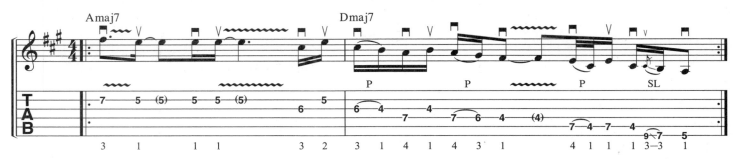

Lick for Shape 2

This lick will help you practice the scale shapes and get you into the groove of slow 16th notes. Notice the half-step bend in measure 1 and the *reverse bend* (also called a *pre-bend*) in 2. When bending, make sure your bent note is precisely in tune. For a half-step bend, compare the bent note to the un-bent note fingered on the next higher fret. They should sound exactly the same. In a reverse bend, the string is bent up before it is plucked, then you release down to the target pitch. Also, notice the slides. The first slide is not picked; it just slides up from the 7th fret to the 10th in the written rhythm. The first note of the second slide, from the 11th fret to the 9th, is picked, but the second note is not.

A Major Scale
Shape 2

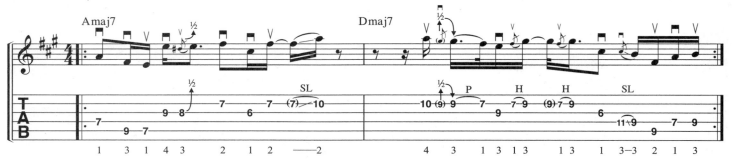

Lick for Shape 3

This lick on Shape 3 works on *tremolo picking* (rapidly repeating a note with alternate picking). When a groove is slow, it's sometimes hard to feel exact subdivisions of the beat before starting your phrase. This lick will help with that. Make sure your vibrato is really wide. You can get another cool sound for this lick by picking closer to the bridge of the guitar for a brighter tone. Remember, any lick can be transposed or truncated to fit any chord in the progression.

A Major Scale
Shape 3

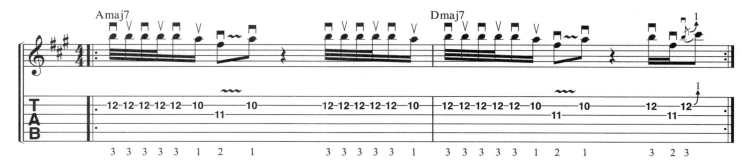

Lick for Shape 4

Again, this lick may look fast but at a slow tempo, you can almost think of the 16th notes as eighth notes at a faster tempo. This lick is all about soul and pocket. It starts with descending 4th *intervals* (the distance between two notes), then the second half of the lick is *double picked* (picking a note twice). It's a great build-up to a hot solo and provides some flash. As you are improvising, experiment with variations. Try making the lick twice as long, elaborating on either the first or second half, switching the order of the two ideas around, or switching the direction of the melodies. Alter as necessary to fit the chord you're playing over.

A Major Scale
Shape 4

11 12 13 14 15

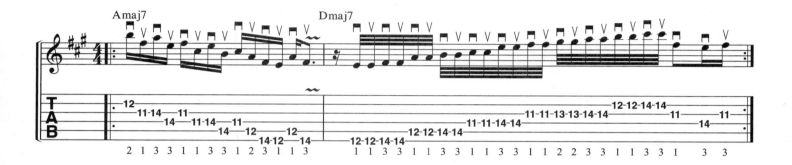

Lick for Shape 5

Here is a lick that moves in wider melodic leaps, which makes for an interesting effect. Solos will often benefit from contrasting ideas: high notes vs. low notes, fast vs. slow, sound vs. silence, repeated ideas vs. new ideas, etc. Try alternating this type of lick with one that doesn't have as much melodic reach. Also, take note of where the slides are in this lick.

A Major Scale
Shape 5

1 2 3 4 5

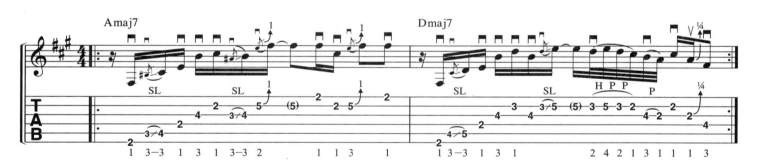

3 BLUE CHECKERBOARD
(Slow Blues-Rock in B♭)

Track 3 (Full Mix)
Track 3A (Minus Guitar Lead)

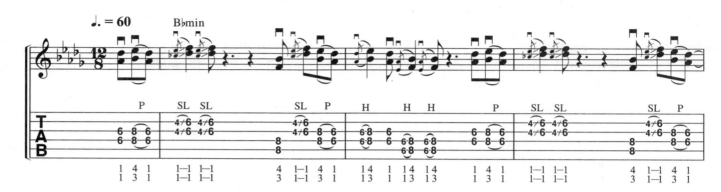

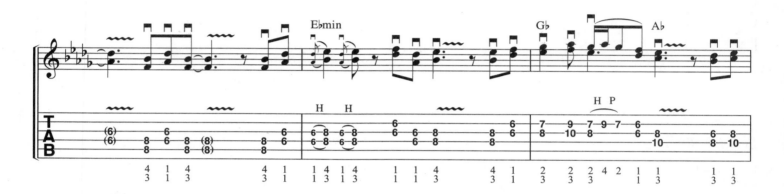

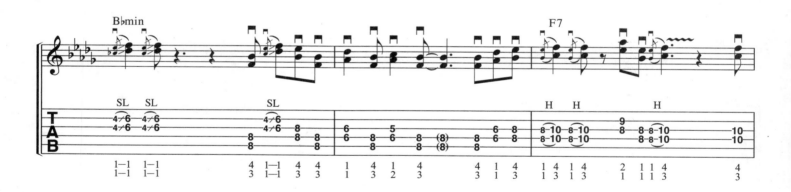

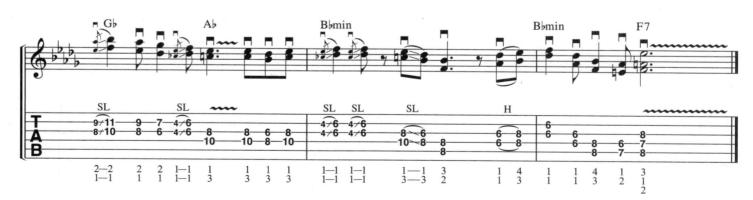

Roadmap

Six total choruses: head, guitar solo (two choruses), keyboard solo, guitar solo, head.

Overview

This song is named after the Checkerboard Lounge, one of the most famous Chicago blues clubs. Started by Buddy Guy in the 1970s, it has hosted such artists as The Rolling Stones, Muddy Waters, and Eric Clapton.

This song is a slow blues-rock—one of the most important styles for guitar players to know. "Blue Checkerboard" is in a traditional 12-bar blues form. Notice the tempo is written as 60 BPM, but the tune is in $\frac{12}{8}$ time. This means the rhythmic current of the song is divided into groups of three, so the dotted quarter note gets one beat. It is similar to playing triplets in $\frac{4}{4}$ time. Thinking of this tune in $\frac{12}{8}$ time will enable you to hear more intricate rhythms within the groove. Once you are familiar with the tune in this key, transpose it into other keys for complete mastery of this style.

- General form: i | i | i | i | iv | VI VII | i | i | V | VI VII | i | i | V
- Key: B♭
- ♩. = 60 BPM

Listening Suggestions

Otis Rush: "Sweet Little Angels"
Check out *All Your Love I Miss Loving: Live at the Wise Fools Pub Chicago* for an authentic recording of how the blues is played. It's important to hear where the blues came from.

Roy Buchanan: "The Messiah Will Come Again"
This is a variation on the 12-bar blues with a minor, almost surf-rock, sound. Roy Buchanan is one of rock's underground guitar heroes and has been a big influence on many well-known rock guitarists, including Jeff Beck, Eric Clapton, and Gary Moore.

Soloing

There are several different chords in this tune (B♭min, E♭min, G♭, A♭, and F7). Let's check out a few different strategies for soloing over these changes.

1. Use the B♭ Minor Blues scale throughout. When chords change, target their roots (B♭, E♭, G♭, A♭, and F)

2. Stay in B♭ Aeolian (Natural Minor) for the whole progression, then switch to B♭ Harmonic Minor for the V (F7) chord.

3. Use the B♭ Minor Blues scale for the i chord (B♭min), E♭ Minor Blues scale for the iv chord (E♭min), E♭ Minor Blues (which is the same as G♭ Major Blues) for the ♭VI (G♭), A♭ Major Blues for the ♭VII (A♭), and F Dominant ♭9 Pentatonic for the V chord (F7).

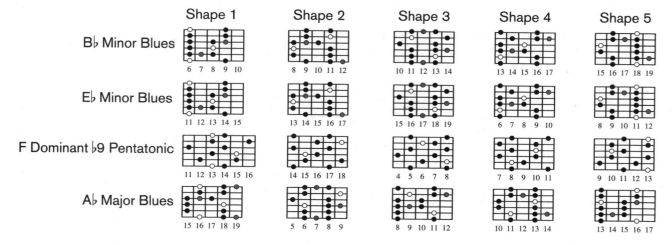

Licks

Lick for Shape 1

Let's focus on getting in the groove. In $\frac{12}{8}$, you need to focus on the steady current of three eighth notes per beat while being aware of the faster rhythms and triplets within that pulse. This lick starts out with some left-hand dampening. The first note is played with the 3rd finger while your 1st finger mutes several strings behind it. The second half of the lick includes several *double stops* (two notes played together). When using this lick in the context of the 12-bar form, try altering it with notes from the other scales to make the chord changes (more in the Soloing section).

B♭ Minor Blues
Shape 1

Lick for Shape 2

This lick focuses on blue notes and further explores the rhythmic possibilities in $\frac{12}{8}$ time. Getting the feel of the rhythms and subdivisions in a slow blues is of the utmost importance. Music from Ghana and Senegal is often written in $\frac{12}{8}$ because of the fast subdivisions. Since the blues was created by early African Americans, it makes sense to explore a slow blues with that in mind.

Notice the bend in measure 1. Bend the 2nd string up a whole step at the 9th fret with your 3rd finger, then sound the same pitch with your 4th finger on the un-bent 11th fret of the same string.

B♭ Minor Blues
Shape 2

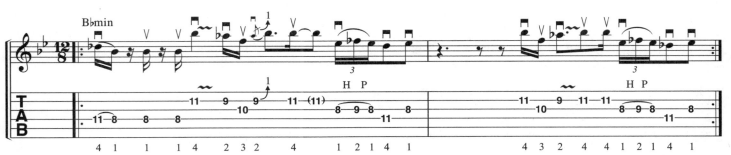

Lick for Shape 3

This lick explores a *pedal point* idea popularized by guitarist Eric Johnson. (The pedal point technique has also been a favorite technique of many Classical and Baroque composers.) In a pedal point, one note stays stationary while the rest of the melody moves around it. Below, the B♭ note is the pedal point against a descending melody. This lick can act as the theme of an entire solo. This technique is a good way to develop a solo and give it special character.

B♭ Minor Blues
Shape 3

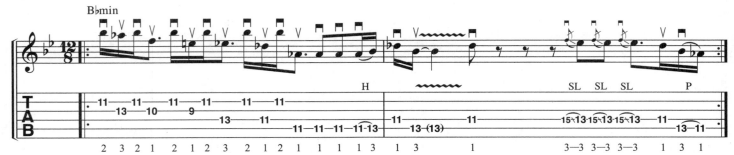

Lick for Shape 4

Notice the 16th-note triplet at the beginning of the lick. A fast triplet figure can spice up your rhythmic phrasing in a slow blues. So why are we talking about playing fast on a slow blues? Here's a wise saying to keep in mind: "If the band plays fast, solo slow. If the band plays slow, solo fast." Keep in mind that contrasting rhythmic phrasing within a solo is generally a good idea at any tempo. Also, notice the held bend on beats 2 and 3 of the first bar. Often, after you bend a note, you may want to do more with the note while it is bent (e.g., applying vibrato, picking the note again, adding tremolo, fretting over the bend, etc.). In this case, the note gets re-picked twice as you hold the bend, then it is released.

B♭ Minor Blues
Shape 4

13 14 15 16 17

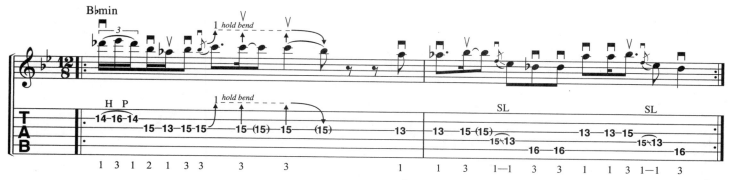

Lick for Shape 5

Here, we are digging even further into the intricate rhythms of a slow blues. This lick will help with your touch. Notes are played with the 1st finger and then muted. Lift your finger very slightly, staying in contact with the string to create a muted note (×) when you pick the string. This type of thing will feel natural with practice.

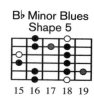

B♭ Minor Blues
Shape 5

15 16 17 18 19

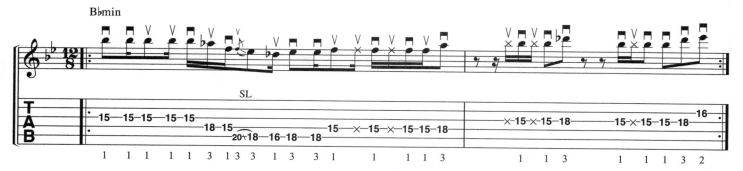

BLIND SWINE
(Hard Rock in B Minor)

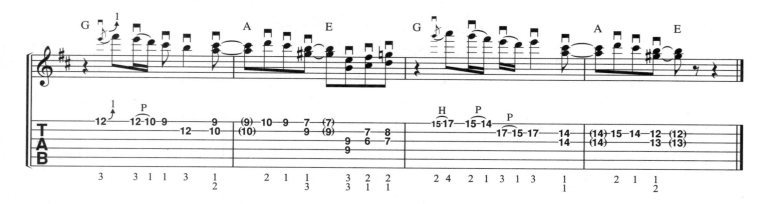

Roadmap

Four total choruses: head, guitar solo, keyboard solo, head plus first four measures of the head as a coda.

Overview

This piece is named after the famous club Blind Pig, which is located in Ann Arbor, Michigan. Sonic Youth, 10,000 Maniacs, Pearl Jam, and Nirvana all played at the Pig when they were just getting started.

This is a 16th-note, hard-rock groove. Use light distortion or a decent amount of overdrive for this melody. Be sure to mute the strings not being played to control the sound. Choose a saturated lead tone for the solo section. The song starts with a rhythm guitar part then jumps into a double-stop melody. The *bridge section* (a contrasting section connecting two main sections) moves to G Major, where the melody shifts between playing double stops and single notes.

- General form: i | VII IV | i | VII | IV, Bridge: ♭VI | VII | IV | ♭VI | VII–IV
- Key: B Minor
- ♩ = 90

<hr>

Listening Suggestions

Van Halen: "I'm the One"
Eddie Van Halen is one of the most influential guitarists of the last century, having transformed the way we view the technique and tone of rock guitar.

Ozzy Osbourne: "Suicide Solution" (Live)
This recording is from the live album *Tribute,* which was released in memory of Randy Rhoads, who played guitar for Ozzy Osbourne from 1979 until his death in 1982. Halfway through the song, Rhoads goes into an unaccompanied solo that is a landmark for modern rock guitar players.

<hr>

Soloing

For most of this song, you can solo using just the B Minor Blues scale or B Dorian. When it goes to the G Major chord (look for it in the last eight bars of the chorus), switch to B Aeolian (to incorporate the G note), but get back to B Dorian for the E Major chord (to incorporate the 3rd of the E chord: G♯).

Licks

B Minor Blues
Shape 1

7 8 9 10 11

Lick for Shape 1

This lick features a popular figure: a descending three-note pattern that is *sequenced* (repeated on different pitch levels). See how that pattern fits in the musical context of this lick.

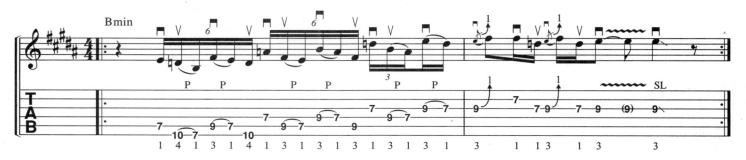

Lick for Shape 2

This lick is both simple and intricate. It starts out with a simple sweep that starts on the & of beat 1. After landing on the tonic (B) with plenty of vibrato, the opening phrase concludes with a short note on beat 2. Notice how this phrase and the following two-note phrase hold over the barline rather than resolve on the *downbeat* (beat 1). This idea of *phrasing over the barline* is highly useful for creating interesting solos.

B Minor Blues
Shape 2

9 10 11 12 13

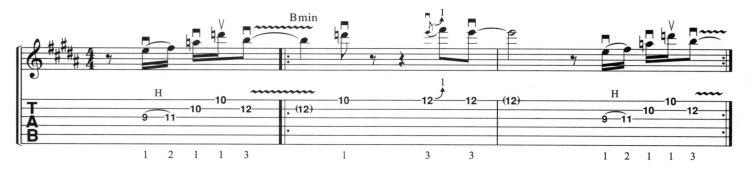

Lick for Shape 3

When there is a 16th-note groove in the rhythm section, it's important for a soloist to be ready with a 16th-note theme that can be repeated. Listeners will immediately recognize that this locks in with the groove.

B Minor Blues
Shape 3

11 12 13 14 15

Lick for Shape 4

We return to simplicity with this next lick, which starts with a soulful, double-stop lick in the first bar. The second bar just rides a rhythm with one note and a few muted hits. To play the phrase, release your left-hand 1st finger from the fret but keep it on the string to stop the note from ringing. Then, play the muted notes by laying your 3rd finger across the strings while plucking the 4th string. With practice, this type of grooving melody riff will come naturally.

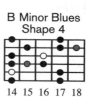

B Minor Blues
Shape 4

14 15 16 17 18

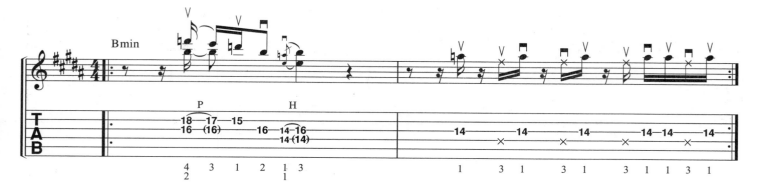

Lick for Shape 5

This lick uses some wider leaps and emphasizes the root note (B). There are two contrasting phrases, one surrounding the root in the lower octave and one hitting it in a higher octave. There is also phrasing over the barline, so as you repeat the phrase, make sure to hold the bent note into the first full bar.

B Minor Blues
Shape 5

4 5 6 7 8

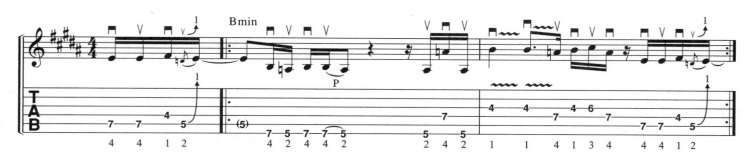

Tipitina's 501

Track 5 (Full Mix)
Track 5A (Minus Guitar Lead)

(Funk Rock in C Minor)

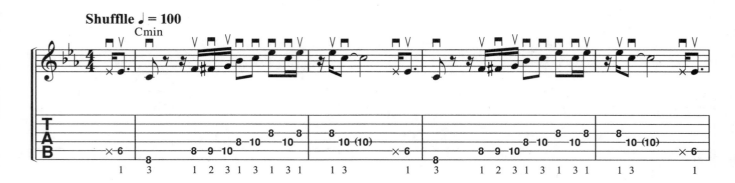

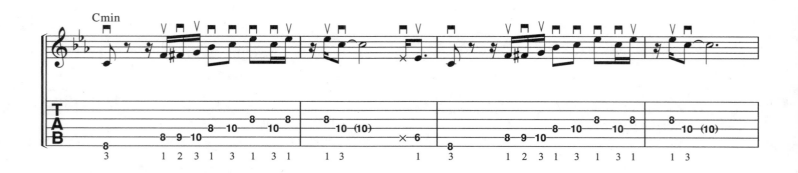

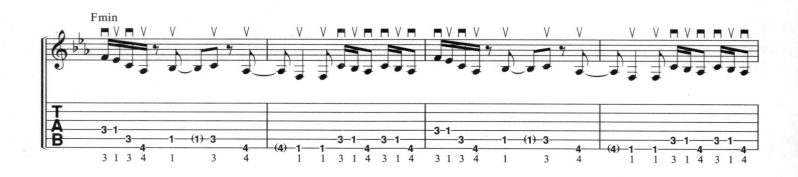

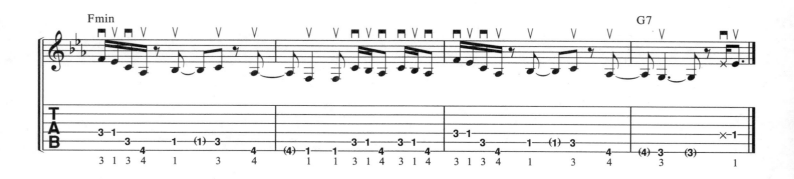

Roadmap

Six total choruses: head, guitar solo, keyboard solo, guitar solo, keyboard solo, head.

Overview

New Orleans is home to an incredible nightclub at 501 Napoleon Avenue called Tipitina's. The bill has always been filled with New Orleans stalwarts like the Funky Meters, Dumpstaphunk, and Trombone Shorty. Traveling bands like Parliament-Funkadelic often make stops there, too.

"Tipitina's 501" is a funk/soul groove with a fast shuffle feel. Instead of straight 16th notes, play with a swing feel that is almost like *sextuplets* (six notes in the time of one beat) but not quite that swung. You could play this tune with light overdrive, a wah-wah pedal, or more distortion to rock it out. Listen to other funk guitarists, and try to get a sense of their sound and feel. Jimi Hendrix played with many soul artists before he became a rock star and was influenced by funk/soul guitarists like Eddie Hazel and Ike Turner who had great lead guitar skills.

- General form: i, Bridge: iv
- Key: C Minor
- ♩ = 100 BPM, Shuffle 16ths

Listening Suggestions

Roy Ayers: "Spirit of Doo Doo"
Calvin Brown was the guitarist on this track, and you can hear how his melodies, grooves, and solos have been highly influential for other funk guitar pioneers.

The Meters: "Cissy Strut"
It's essential for every guitarist to know this funk tune. It is commonly requested at jam sessions, and artists like John Scofield and John Mayer have played it in their sets. The Meters were a very successful backing band for soul and funk artists in the South. Meters guitarist Leo Nocentelli helped define the sound of New Orleans funk.

Soloing

The two sections in this song have two basic tonalities: C Minor and F Minor. To keep your soloing ideas simple, just use minor blues and Dorian, and remember to switch keys for the chord change. Here are the scale shapes:

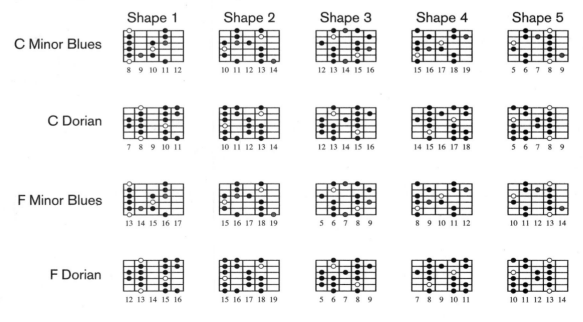

Licks

Licks for Shape 1

Shape 1 of the minor blues scale is always a great home base for blues and rock guitarists. This lick will give you a sweet, funky phrase to incorporate into many different styles. It can also make a strong melody when looped around over the changes. Notice that it does go out of Shape 1 at the end of the first measure. It is common to use notes from neighboring shapes, even when the same notes are available in the original shape, because the neighboring shapes will give you a different sound when played in another position on a different string.

C Minor Blues
Shape 1

8 9 10 11 12

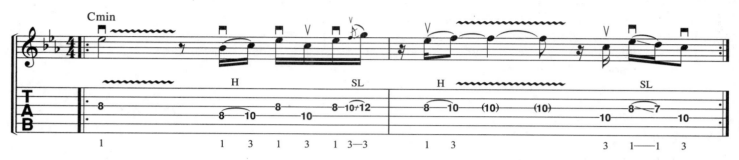

This lick explores a great, repeatable pentatonic pattern in found in Shape 1. The pattern ascends three notes through the scale and then leaps up a 4th. It is then sequenced, starting on each subsequent note of the scale. The mix of close notes and leaps is an interesting effect. Repeat this until you can play it quickly and comfortably.

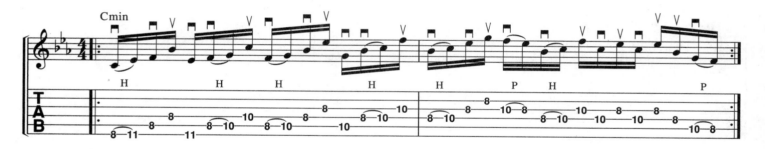

Licks for Shape 2

In this lick, we slide to the second degree of the scale (borrowed from C Dorian) and then resolve to the root. The three-note lick in the second measure is repeated down an octave (with the last note reaching out of the shape). Experiment with transposing some other licks, or small pieces of them, by an octave.

C Minor Blues
Shape 2

10 11 12 13 14

This next lick is also in Shape 2 but including more range. Take note of the vibrato, hammer-ons, pull-offs, and slides. Locking these 16th notes into the groove is key. Practice this lick by looping it around until you have it memorized. Eventually, you will want to be able to just pick up the guitar and pull it off in perfect time.

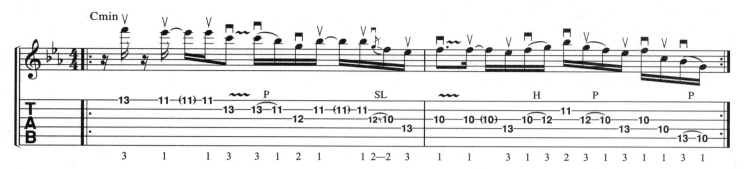

Licks for Shape 3

This lick uses octave leaps in Shape 3. This idea is cool any way you play it but if you can pull this off in time, it's such a fresh idea that audiences will be caught off guard in a good way. The beginning of the second measure features a unison bend: the 16th-fret bend on the 2nd string and the following un-bent 13th-fret note on the 1st string ring out together and sound the same pitch. There is a reverse bend at the end of the lick where the note is bent before it is picked. After being picked, it is released back to its unaltered pitch.

C Minor Blues
Shape 3

12 13 14 15 16

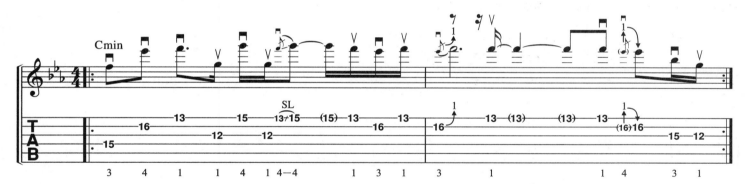

This lick starts out with a quick, 16th-note bend and then hits the un-bent note immediately after. The rhythm is very *syncopated* (off-beat: the accent is shifted to a weak beat or a weak part of a beat), so take it slow and make sure each rhythm is precise. Notice the slide down to the 15th fret at the start of the second measure. The note at the 15th fret is F, the 4th, and sliding to the 4th of the scale is common. Keep in mind that when you transition to the bridge section, you should change from C Minor to F Minor.

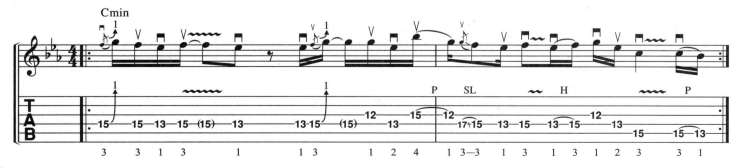

Licks for Shape 4

Here's another funky, syncopated lead melody. Try picking close to the bridge of the guitar to get a bright tone, even if you have the neck pickup selected.

Once you get the sound of this lick into your head and have it memorized, try varying it by altering just the first bar and keeping the second bar as written, or vice versa.

C Minor Blues
Shape 4

15 16 17 18 19

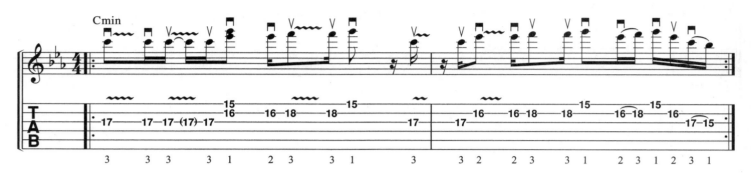

Since we are dealing with funk here, incorporating a jazz vocabulary could work. This lick is inspired by saxophonist Eddie Harris and guitarist John Scofield, who both frequently use leaps of a 4th in their lines.

This pattern includes alternating ascending and descending 4ths, which is sometimes called *flipping*. The pentatonic scale and the blues scale are largely made up of 4ths, so this technique and sound should come naturally to most guitarists.

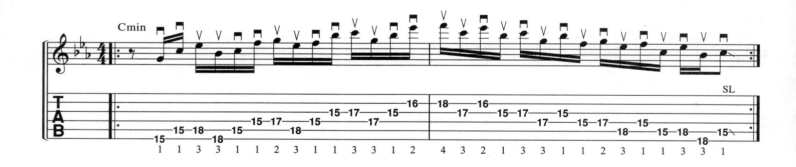

Licks for Shape 5

Here is a funky repeated phrase that puts the focus on slides. There are slides leading up to and down to notes.

When playing slides, it is common to start about two frets away from the targeted note, either above or below, then slide into the target pitch as soon as you strike the string with your pick.

C Minor Blues
Shape 5

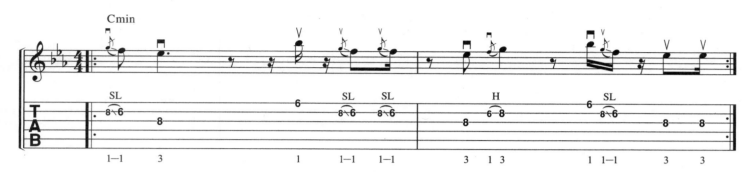

Compared to the other licks you've been playing, the next lick is relatively simple—in terms of rhythm and technique. Don't let that fool you, though. Sometimes simplicity is where it's at.

Here's something to keep in mind: After or before you play something elaborate, try to play some simple melodies that stick to the groove and lock the band's sound together. It's another example of contrast that can make what you play memorable.

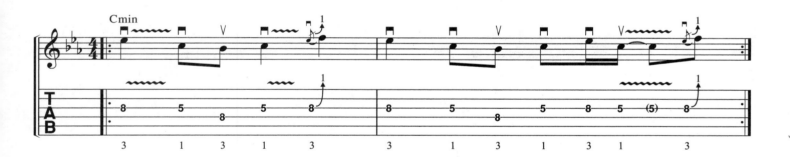

Track 6 (Full Mix)
Track 6A (Minus Guitar Lead)

BREAKING LIMITS
(Country Rock in C# Minor)

Roadmap

Seven total choruses: 8-measure intro, head, keyboard solo, guitar solo, keyboard solo, guitar solo, head.

Overview

Austin City Limits (ACL) should need no introduction. As a venue, festival, and TV show, its influence is vast. The beautiful Moody Theater has been home to this major music series since the early 1970s. Originally created for country and blues, ACL has gone on to represent every genre of popular music.

This tune is a blend of a steady eighth-note rock feel in the style of U2 and country pop-rock playing. It features double stops, triple stops, and *country bending* (a unique bending technique that comes from imitating country and bluegrass instruments, such as the banjo, dobro, and pedal steel guitar). Country guitar styles are found in Southern rock, and it has become an in-demand style for the modern studio guitarist.

- General form: i | ♭VI | ♭III | ♭VII, Chorus: ♭VI | ♭III | ♭VII | ♭VII
- Key: C♯ Minor
- ♩ = 105 BPM

Listening Suggestions

Hellecasters: "Back on Terra Firma & Sweet Dreams"
The Hellecasters are one of the most popular country guitar groups. With three top-notch players ripping in harmony and trading solos, they keep everyone on the edge of their seat.

John Mayer: "Belief"
Modern country music might seem far away from pop artists like John Mayer, but both could be viewed under the Americana umbrella. This is a great song that nails the feel we intend for "Breaking Limits."

Carrie Underwood: "Blown Away"
This is the most un-guitaristic song in the book, but it's a great modern country-pop reference. The feel is not rooted in country but, rather, a rock four-on-the-floor feel.

Soloing

In this chapter, we'll discuss country-style techniques you can use to spice up your solos. This will create a country flavor, but be sure to try them in other styles of music. This tune is in the key of C♯ Minor, so you can use the C♯ Natural Minor scale, the C♯ Minor Blues scale, and lots of open strings (E, B, A, and low E) in your soloing. The licks are in *closed position* (no open strings, usually involving about five adjacent frets), so they can be easily transposed to other keys.

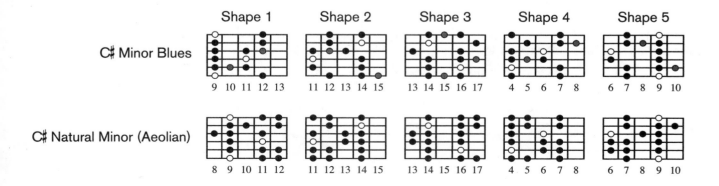

Licks

Licks for Shape 1

Hybrid picking, often called called *chicken pickin'*, is a popular country guitar technique. In this technique, many—if not all—upstrokes of the pick are replaced by a percussive upward fingerpick with the middle finger, ring finger, or pinky. Pulling the string upward with a right-hand finger causes the string to slap back down on the frets, creating a percussive effect.

This first lick is going to help you get your hybrid picking together. It can be played with either *broken alternate picking* (down–up–down, down–up–down) or with hybrid picking (ring–middle–down-pick). This basic *roll* (repeated right-hand pattern) may seem awkward at first, but with practice you'll be able to perform it with an ease similar to that of great banjo fingerpickers.

C# Minor Blues
Shape 1

9 10 11 12 13

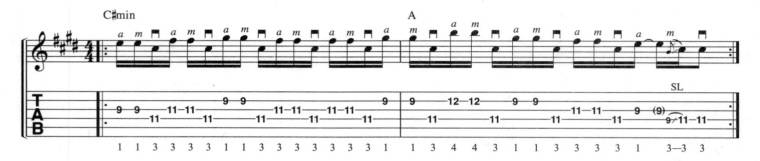

To play this funky lick, use your middle finger to pick all of the notes on the 3rd string to give it some of that country-funk tone.

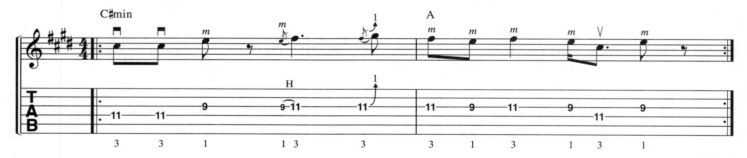

Licks for Shape 2

This lick can be played with either *sweep picking* (playing consecutive notes on adjacent strings with one fluid downstroke or upstroke) or with hybrid picking. It's important to experiment to find the way that feels right for you. For example, using beat 2 as a reference, either use:

C# Minor Blues
Shape 2

11 12 13 14 15

- Sweep Picking: Down–down–hammer-on–up–up–pull-off, or
- Hybrid Picking: Down–middle–hammer-on–ring–middle–pull-off

Use your chosen technique for the rest of the lick. The first lick for Shape 2 begins on the following page.

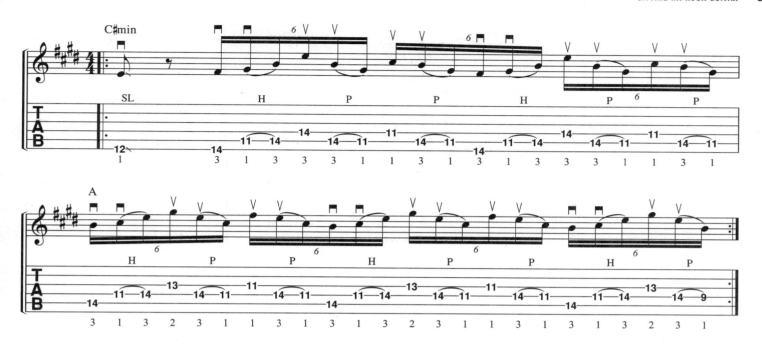

Within a straight-pop feel, it's sometimes fun to solo with an idea that spices up the rhythm and adds syncopation.

This is an opportunity to use *rhythmic superimposition*, which is where a one rhythm is played over another. Here, we are playing straight 16th notes (four notes to the beat) but phrasing it in groups of five, which causes the first note of the pattern (high G♯) to be displaced (moved to a different part of the beat) each time it is played.

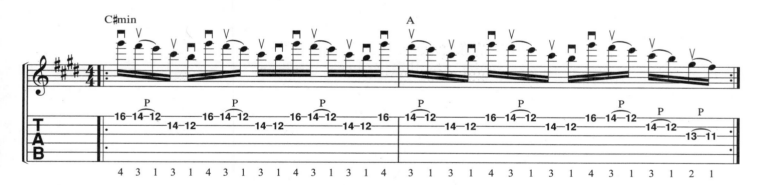

Licks for Shape 3

C♯ Minor Blues
Shape 3

13 14 15 16 17

Here is a bluesy bending lick for Shape 3. It uses a quick 16th-note triplet to help break up the phrasing of the 16th notes.

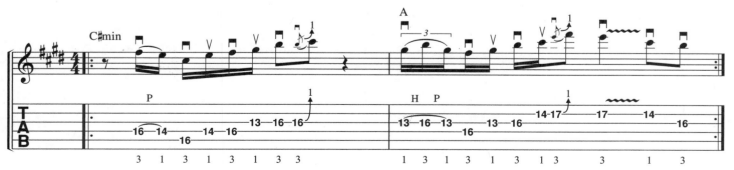

This lick uses left-hand dampening to create some funky muted notes. This will help with establishing finesse and touch in your playing. Practice playing one note at a time, lifting your finger just enough to mute the string.

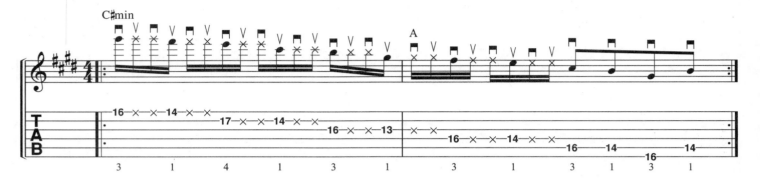

Licks for Shape 4

This lick features sweep picking, bending, and hammer-on *ornaments* (notes that embellish a melody). The sweep-picking phrase at the beginning of the lick is played with all downstrokes, with each stroke resting on the next string. The quick up-bend has no release.

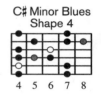

C# Minor Blues
Shape 4

4 5 6 7 8

Next, play the hammer-on ornaments with a quick *flam* (a drum rudiment where a quick embellishment is played directly before the main note) effect.

This lick also uses Shape 4, but it features many more chromatic notes. One of the easiest ways to add depth to your playing is to fill in the spaces between the notes of scales, such as pentatonic and blues scales with *chromatic passing tones* (a passing tone is a non-chord tone inserted between chord tones).

Check out the *legato* (smoothly connected notes, usually accomplished with hammer-ons or pull-offs) phrases within this lick.

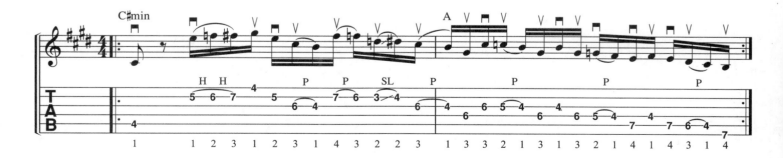

Licks for Shape 5

Let's explore more tremolo picking with the minor blues scale in Shape 5. This lick will get you into the feel of sextuplets at a moderate tempo. When used in conjunction with other licks, it's important to keep the sextuplet rhythmic subdivisions in the back of your mind, so that the transitions in and out of them are smooth.

Also, experiment with picking this at different locations on the strings—close to, or further from, the bridge.

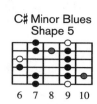

C# Minor Blues
Shape 5

6 7 8 9 10

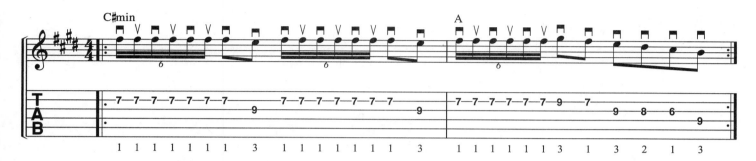

Here is a faster picking lick that you can play with either strict alternate picking, or, preferably, *economy picking*. With economy picking, the rule is this: alternate pick when multiple notes in a row are on the same string, but when you move down a string, pick down; when you move up a string, pick up.

In this example, the picking for the first beat is: down–up–down–down–up–down.

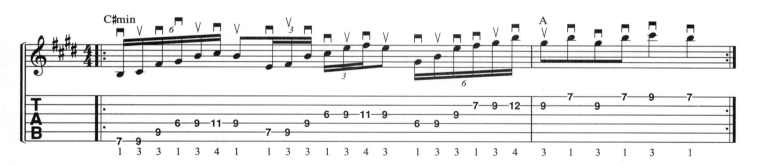

Track 7 (Full Mix)
Track 7A (Minus Guitar Lead)

CROCODILE IN THE RAIN
(Alternative Rock in D Minor)

Roadmap

Six total choruses: head A, head B, keyboard solo (full chorus), guitar solo (two choruses), head B.

Overview

The title of this piece refers to the Crocodile Cafe, now just known as the Crocodile, in Seattle, WA, where groups like Nirvana, Pearl Jam, Alice in Chains, Mudhoney, and the Posies developed their sound.

This song is in *Drop D tuning,* so tune your low-E string down a whole step. Also, it follows a 16-bar minor blues form.

- General form: i | i | i | i | i | i | i | i | i | iv | iv | i | i | v | iv | i | i
- Key: D Minor
- ♩. = 105

Listening Suggestions

Soundgarden: "Outshined"
The main Drop D riff by guitarist Kim Thayil is one of the signatures of grunge rock.

Pearl Jam: "Even Flow"
Here's another classic Drop D riff in the context of a great song. Guitarists Stone Gossard and Mike McCready helped define the sound of Pearl Jam and a generation of music.

Soloing

For this song, use D Minor Blues or D Natural Minor for the i chord, G Minor Blues or G Dorian for the iv chord, and A Minor Blues or A Phrygian for the v chord.

Licks

D Minor Blues
Shape 1

10 11 12 13 14

Lick for Shape 1

The first lick starts out with an ascending arpeggio leading into some unison bends.

Lick for Shape 2

D Minor Blues
Shape 2

12 13 14 15 16

This lick features three kinds of bends: a quarter-step bend (just bend the string up a little bit, less than a half step, for emphasis); a one-and-a-half-step bend that takes a good amount of strength; and a whole-step bend, re-pick, and release to conclude.

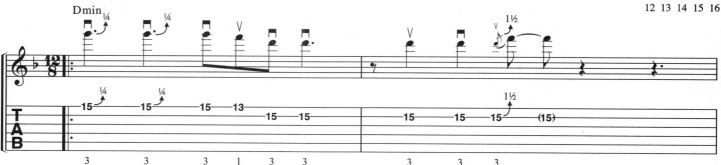

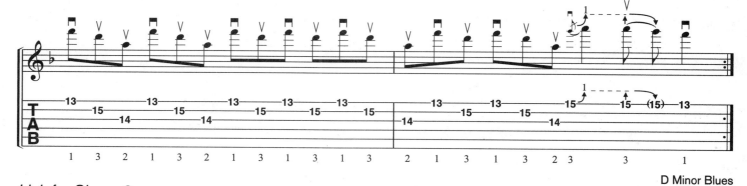

Lick for Shape 3

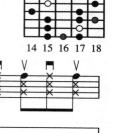

D Minor Blues
Shape 3

14 15 16 17 18

Here is a left-hand dampening lick where your 3rd and 4th fingers rest across the strings while your 1st finger plays the fretted notes.

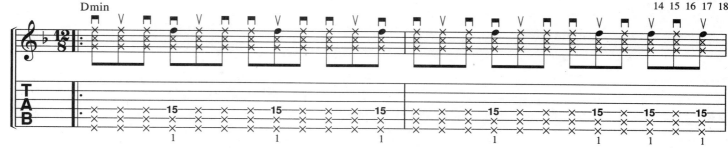

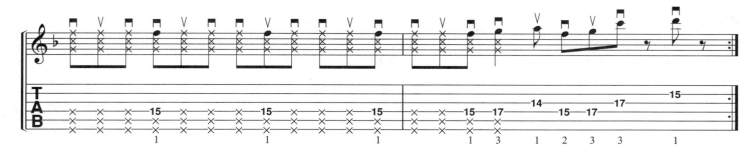

Lick for Shape 4

Here is a lick that explores rhythmic superimposition in $\frac{12}{8}$ time. This lick uses four-note phrasing superimposed over three-note groupings of $\frac{12}{8}$ time.

D Minor Blues
Shape 4

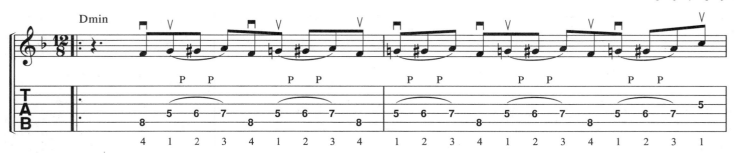

Lick for Shape 5

This lick explores *theme and variation phrasing* using different starting beats. The theme begins in bar 1, beat 2, and the first variation is in bar 2; it is higher and starts on beat 1. The next two bars feature a variation of this theme by extending the melody.

D Minor Blues
Shape 5

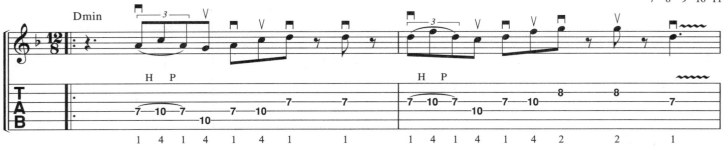

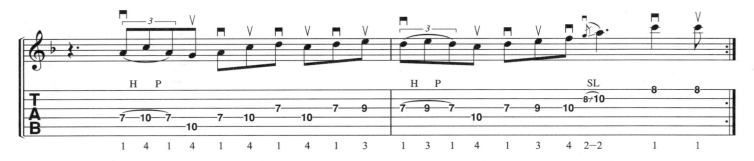

PROTECTOR OF MUSIC

Track 8 (Full Mix)
Track 8A (Minus Guitar Lead)

(Funk Rock in Eb Minor)

Roadmap

Five total choruses: head, guitar solo, keyboard solo, guitar solo, head.

Overview

The Apollo Theater in New York City isn't just a nightclub, it's an institution with a rich history of acts like the Staple Singers, Sam Cooke with the Soul Stirrers, Ray Charles, Otis Redding, and Aretha Franklin. Apollo is the Greek god of music, and this song, "Protector of Music," honors the Apollo Theater.

This song has three sections, each with a separate groove. Soul, funk, and disco music will often stay on a groove for awhile and then transition into another contrasting groove. James Brown used to yell to his saxophone player, "Maceo, take me to the bridge!" to hype up the next section before it hit.

Notice that the three sections are labeled A, B, and C. The A section is all double stops. Just let the first note (the dotted half notes) of each two-bar phrase ring out. This puts a strong accent on beat 1, which is common in funk and soul music. The rest of the lick dances around that hit on beat 1. Section B is a descending progression of 16th-note strums. Make sure this is locked into the pocket and together with the band. Practice with a metronome to master this, making sure that the first and last note of each 16th-note flurry is perfectly in the pocket. Section C is a unison line with the bass guitar. This type of groove is great for building up tension in a jam. Enjoy!

- General form: Section A: i | v iv, Section B: i | ♭VII | ♭VI | V, Section C: i
- Key: E♭ Minor
- ♩ = 120 BPM

Listening Suggestions

James Brown: "Get Up (I Feel Like Being a) Sex Machine"
The dynamic duo of bassist William "Bootsy" Collins and rhythm guitarist Phelps "Catfish" Collins, who are also brothers, added tons of groove to this track. James Brown was certainly one of the most influential figures in all things groove-related.

Sly and the Family Stone: "Sing a Simple Song"
When Sly and the Family Stone hit Woodstock in 1969, they made their mark. Their sound featured a mix of soul, funk, and psychedelic rock via guitarist Freddie Stone.

Curtis Mayfield: "Superfly"
This song is from the soundtrack to a movie with the same title. Curtis Mayfield's guitar and vocal style is instantly identifiable.

Soloing

For soloing on this tune, stick to the E♭ Minor Blues scale and E♭ Natural Minor. Here are the scale shapes:

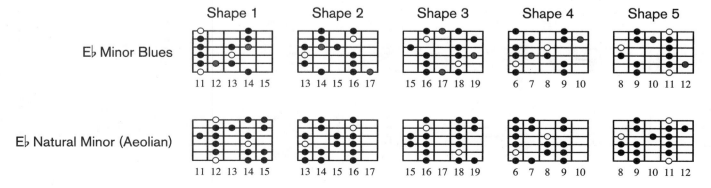

Licks

Lick for Shape 1

This lick features a little trick at the end: the 16th-triplet section uses a *rolling* technique to smoothly move across the strings. Start by fingering with the tip of your 1st finger, then hammer on the next note. When you pull off, collapse the tip joint a little and land on the pad of your 1st finger. Now, the 1st finger rolls down to play the next string with the tip again; repeat. This rolling effect is fast and efficient and will feel as though the finger is just shimmying up or down the strings.

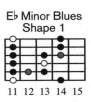

Eb Minor Blues
Shape 1

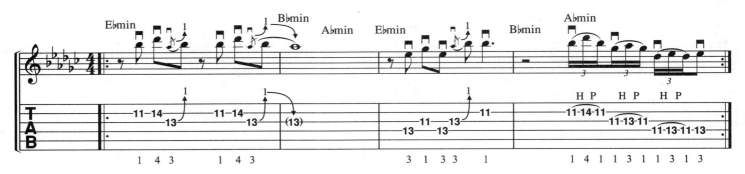

Lick for Shape 2

When soloing in a funk-rock groove, it's great to use ornaments like those demonstrated in this next lick. These quick little hammer-ons and pull-offs dress up a melody with bit of soul.

Eb Minor Blues
Shape 2

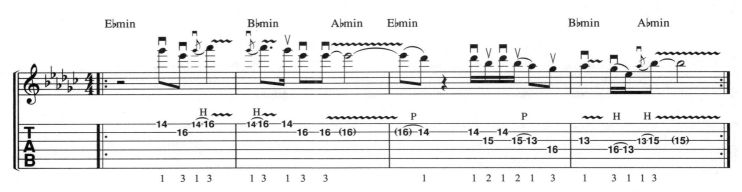

Lick for Shape 3

Let's explore Shape 3 with a catchy repeated rhythm. This melody moves down in a natural-feeling one-and-a-half-beat phrase, which gives a nice syncopated onbeat–offbeat–onbeat, push–pull effect. As with many of the licks in this book, this phrasing idea was played naturally and then put under a microscope, not the other way around. Once you get this concept into your head and hands, it should become a natural soloing concept for you.

Eb Minor Blues
Shape 3

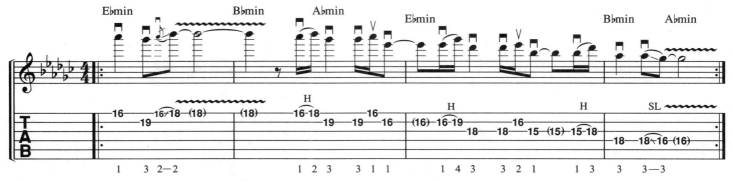

Licks for Shape 4

Here is a lick with a bluesy soul groove and some cool bending techniques. The first two notes illustrate an important technique. Bend the first note up a whole step, then pick it again and add vibrato. When vibrato is added to this already bent note, you get a downward vibrato, scooping below the note, unlike typical vibrato that rocks above. In the blues, this is often referred to as the *crying effect*.

Eb Minor Blues
Shape 4

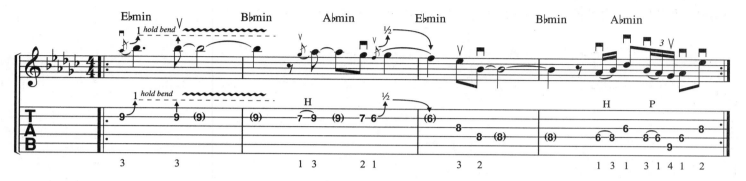

Lick for Shape 5

This lick might feature some tricky rhythm and phrasing, but don't shy away from it. The lick brings to mind some of the lead lines from the Rail Band, a 1970s funk group from Mali, Africa. Their guitarist, Djelimady Tounkara, is excellent and often performs interval leaps with offbeat grooves like the ones here.

Eb Minor Blues
Shape 5

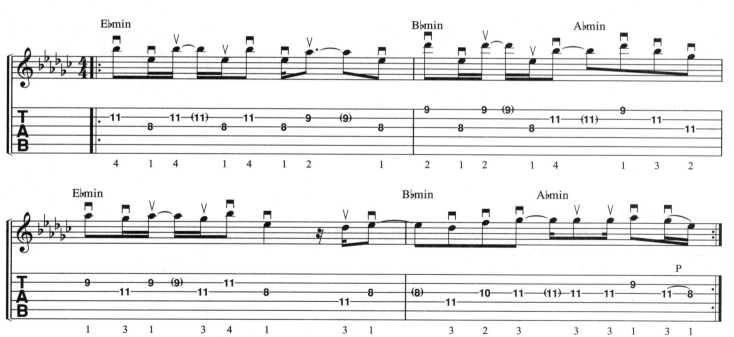

ECHOES IN THE CAVERN
(Blues-Rock in E)

Swing ♩ = 120

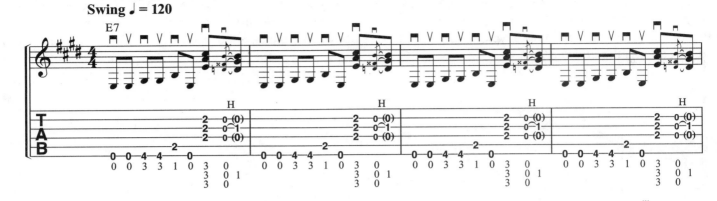

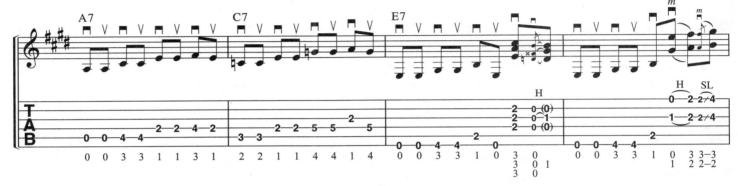

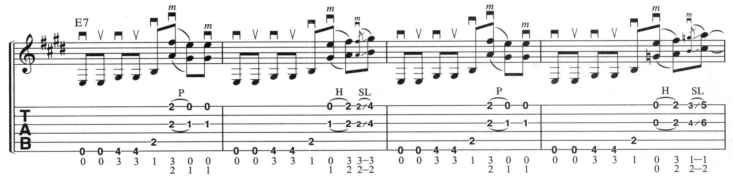

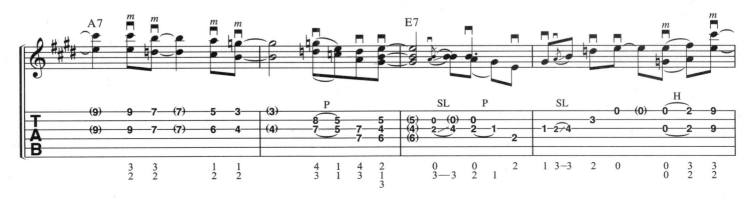

Roadmap

Five total choruses: head, guitar solo, keyboard solo, guitar solo, head.

Overview

The Cavern Club in Liverpool, England, is one of the most famous venues in the world. It's the club that started The Beatles, Elton John, The Rolling Stones, Queen, The Yardbirds, and more-recent acts like The Arctic Monkeys, Travis, The Wanted, and Adele. This piece is reminiscent of the early British blues sound of the Cavern's heyday.

The major difference between the notation of this song and previous songs in this book is its use of *swing eighths*. This means the rhythmic current is triplets, similar to how we played in ¹²⁄₈ on previous songs. Often in blues and jazz, instead of being written in ¹²⁄₈ time, this feel is written in ₄⁄₄ with a "Swing" marking at the start of the piece. When a tune is marked "Swing," the eighth notes are played as a triplet with the first two notes tied.

Swing Eighths

- General form: Verse: I | I | I | I | IV | ♭VI, Chorus: VI | VI | I | I | VI | VI | V | V
- Key: E Major
- ♩ = 120 BPM, Swing 8ths

Listening Suggestions

The Beatles: "Dig a Pony"
Choosing only one Beatles song is difficult, because they have so many great tunes. A good starting place to check out this song is the footage of them playing it at their famous rooftop concert on the top of Apple Studios on Savile Row in London.

The Yardbirds: "Jeff's Blues"
The Yardbirds are an important guitar group to know about because they featured three of British rock's greatest guitarists: Eric Clapton, Jimmy Page, and, as featured in this song, Jeff Beck.

Soloing

For soloing over this tune, use either the E Minor Blues scale, the E Major Blues scale, or E Mixolydian on the I chord (E7). For the IV chord (A7) use either the home key E Minor Blues, A Major Blues scale, or B Mixolydian. For the V (B7), use B Minor Blues or B Mixolydian. Please refer to the appendix on page 78 for the scale shapes used throughout.

Licks

Lick for Shape 1

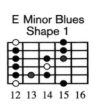

E Minor Blues
Shape 1

12 13 14 15 16

This first lick illustrates the contrast between riding the triplet motion and a faster sextuplet flurry. The sliding lick in bars 3 and 4 might look tricky, but it is a great effect that is easily achieved by hammering-on, pulling-off, and sliding your 1st finger back and forth.

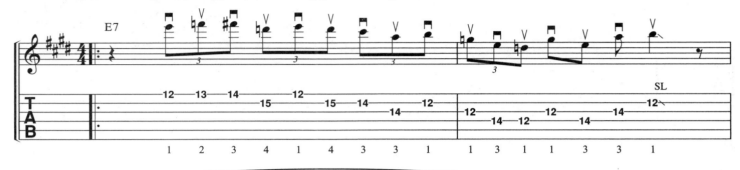

Lick for Shape 2

E Minor Blues
Shape 2

2 3 4 5 6

For Shape 2, try this 16th-note triplet phrase. Keep in mind that the eighth note preceding each triplet is still swung. The slides are performed by starting two frets away and then sliding directly into the destination fret.

Lick for Shape 3

E Minor Blues
Shape 3

4 5 6 7 8

This soulful blues lick starts with a half-step bend from the 9th of the key to the 10th (or: the 2nd to the 3rd, up an octave). It outlines E Dorian and needs plenty of vibrato.

Lick for Shape 4

This lick uses a classic blues lead technique built around Shape 4. It focuses on sliding *6ths* (notes that are six steps apart). This sound is quite common in rock, blues, and soul guitar styles. Repeat this lick until it feels natural enough to incorporate into your own improvisation.

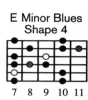

E Minor Blues
Shape 4

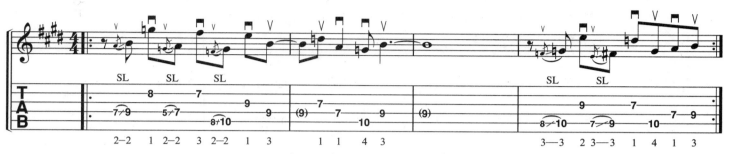

Lick for Shape 5

Here's a classic fast lick that will help you feel sextuplets in a swing groove and improve your chops. Take note of which notes are picked and which aren't. This is the most important aspect of this lick: the mixture of legato and staccato in a quick phrase. Also, we are combining notes from two shapes (Shapes 1 and 5) here, which creates a wider stretch for your hand but gives you new fingering possibilities for blues and pentatonic scales.

E Minor Blues
Shape 5

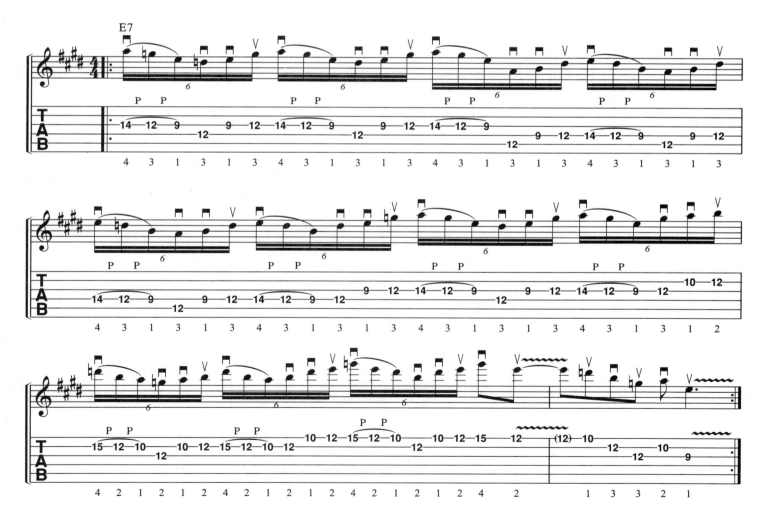

WANDERING TROUBADOUR
(Hard Rock in F Lydian)

Track 10 (Full Mix)
Track 10A (Minus Guitar Lead)

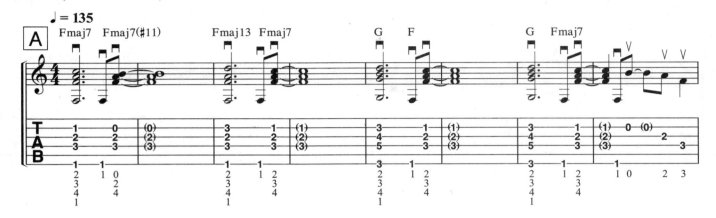

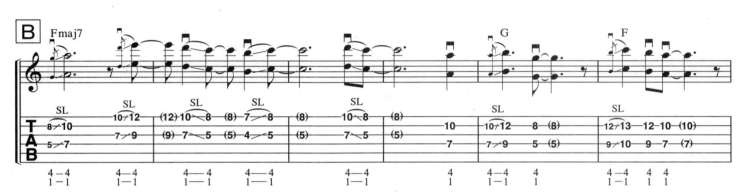

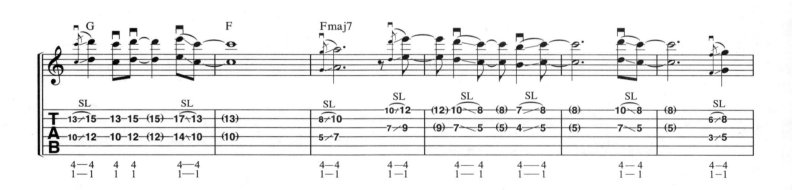

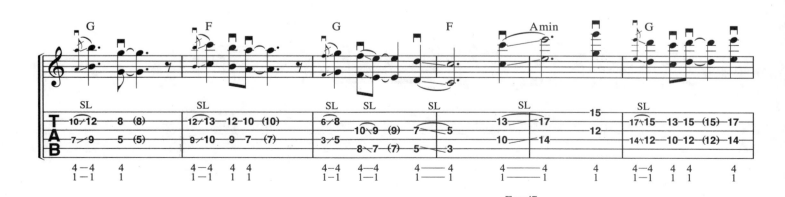

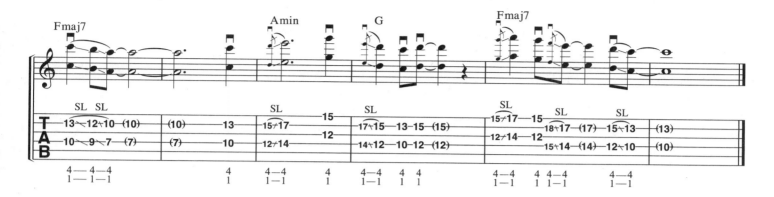

Roadmap

Seven total choruses: head A, head B, guitar solo, keyboard solo, guitar solo, keyboard solo, head B.

Overview

The Troubadour in West Hollywood, CA has been instrumental in launching the careers of many great artists, including Elton John, James Taylor, Carole King, Tom Waits, Joni Mitchell, The Byrds, Jackson Browne, Neil Diamond, Guns N' Roses, and the Eagles. This song is inspired by both the songwriters and the hard rock acts that have appeared at that venue.

"Wandering Troubadour" uses the Lydian mode, which is made up of the same notes as the major scale but beginning from the fourth degree. It has a floating, dreamy sound.

- General form: I | I | I | I | II | I | II | I Bridge iii | II | I | I
- Key: F Lydian
- ♩ = 135 BPM

Listening Suggestions

Joe Satriani: "Flying in a Blue Dream"
This is one of the most famous guitar songs in Lydian, and it's performed by one of the most important instrumental rock guitarists of all time, Joe Satriani.

Bjork: "Possibly Maybe"
Here is another showcase of Lydian. While this song does not incorporate guitar, it is a great example of modern pop production.

Soloing

This song stays in F Lydian the entire time, so the F Lydian scale will work over the whole chart. However, the D Minor Pentatonic or D Blues scale will work well on this tune. So if that is more comfortable, use it instead. Please refer to the appendix on page 78 for the scale shapes used throughout.

Licks

Lick for Shape 1

The licks in this section use the D Minor Pentatonic scale, and that scale's relationship to the key of F is important to understand. When playing in most major tonalities, including major (Ionian), Mixolydian, and Lydian, you can solo using the minor pentatonic scale that is three frets lower than your tonic. Even over this new Lydian soundscape, the familiar minor pentatonic scale should make you feel right at home.

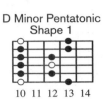

D Minor Pentatonic
Shape 1

10 11 12 13 14

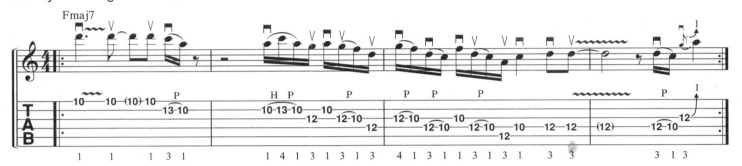

Lick for Shape 2

The next lick is inspired by the great legato playing of Joe Satriani. Here, we are adding some Lydian notes that are missing from the pentatonic scale. Notice how these notes relate to the pentatonic shape. Also, notice that the third measure features a bend that is picked again while bent and then picked a third time for the release.

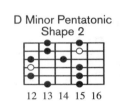

D Minor Pentatonic
Shape 2

12 13 14 15 16

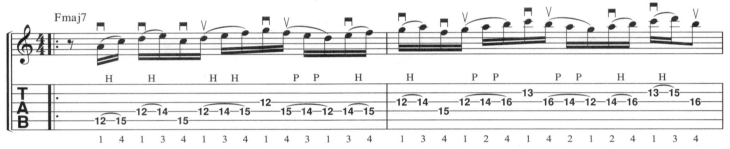

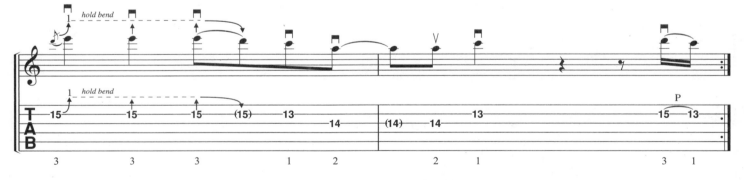

Lick for Shape 3

Mastering this kind of repetitive-pattern lick is a great way to help your solos fall right into the pocket of the band. This lick repeats in a three-against-four rhythmic superimposition (16th notes phrased in threes). The pattern builds up the scale and ends triumphantly with vibrato.

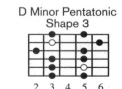

D Minor Pentatonic
Shape 3

2 3 4 5 6

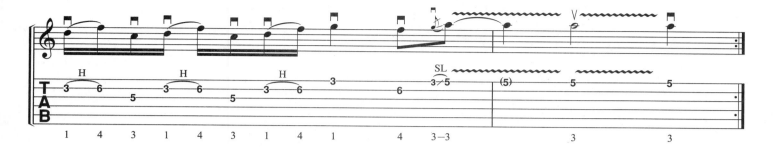

Lick for Shape 4

This lick features a pattern of threes through the scale. However, rather than fretting each note, the first note is bent up to the second one, and then the third note is picked. This pattern continues through to bar 2 and resolves into bar 3. The lick finishes off with a blues-scale legato lick.

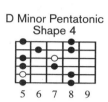

D Minor Pentatonic
Shape 4

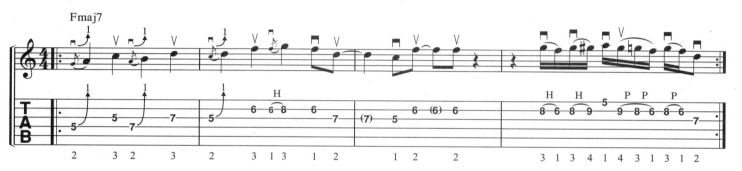

Lick for Shape 5

This last lick features some sweep and economy picking licks that are phrased to give just a bit more flash and flavor to the otherwise bluesy sound of the phrase.

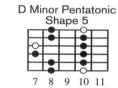

D Minor Pentatonic
Shape 5

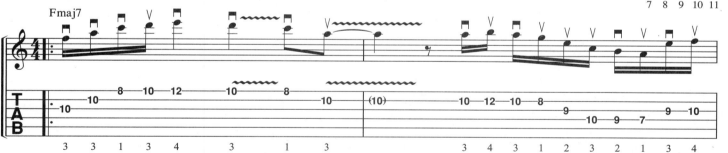

80 Proof to Go
(Heavy Metal in F#)

Track 11 (Full Mix)
Track 11A (Minus Guitar Lead)

Roadmap

Riff A, riff B (four times), riff A, riff B (four times), riff C (four times), riff D (four times), riff A, riff B (four times), riff A, riff B (four times), riff C (four times), riff D (four times).

Overview

The Whisky a Go Go is an iconic club on the Sunset Strip in Hollywood, CA. Many rock icons got their start there, including The Doors, The Byrds, Buffalo Springfield, Alice Cooper, Frank Zappa, Motley Crüe, Red Hot Chili Peppers, System of a Down, and many other hard rock and heavy metal bands. The Whisky has been known primarily as a hard rock and metal venue in the modern era, and that is the style of our tune, "80 Proof to Go."

This metal composition features several riffs and sections that you should play with attitude and intensity. Check out the recording to hear how the band arranges these four sections. The key of this tune is F♯ Phrygian. The Phrygian mode is the same notes as the major scale but starting from the third degree. In other words, F♯ Phrygian is made up of the same notes as D Major. Definitely crank on some distortion for this track and let it rip.

- Key: F♯ Phrygian
- ♩ = 145 BPM

Listening Suggestions

Death: "The Philosopher"
Chuck Schuldiner, guitarist, vocalist, and mastermind of Death, helped start extreme metal. One of the most important aspects of playing in metal styles is locking in with the band and having your rhythm chops together. Listen to this track to hear how easily it changes tempos.

Judas Priest: "Breaking the Law"
Judas Priest helped start heavy metal and this track, while having a classic sound, is a metal anthem that will stand the test of time. Guitarists K. K. Downing and Glenn Tipton helped define the sound of heavy metal.

Metallica: "Master of Puppets"
There are so many great tracks from Metallica's early days, and this is certainly one of their most iconic songs. Guitarists James Hetfield and Kirk Hammett paved the way for the guitar metal revolution.

Megadeth: "Peace Sells...but Who's Buying?"
Megadeth was started by former Metallica guitarist Dave Mustaine. Their sound, featuring lyrics about politics and religion, fast guitar riffs, and complex arrangements, is distinct from other thrash bands

Soloing

For soloing on this song, use F♯ Minor Blues or F♯ Phrygian throughout the form. Here are those two scales and their scale shapes for you to check out:

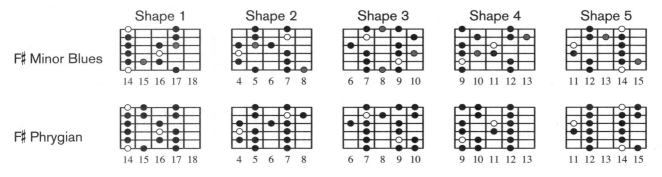

Licks

Licks for Shape 1

This first lick is long for the sake of development and is an example of a lead break as an interlude section, a common heavy metal convention. Here, a hammer-on phrase shifts notes through the scale for harmonic development. Try it slow at first, and let it rip once you have it down.

F# Minor Blues
Shape 1

14 15 16 17 18

This lick is also in Shape 1 and features intricate bending phrases like those found in many metal guitar solos.

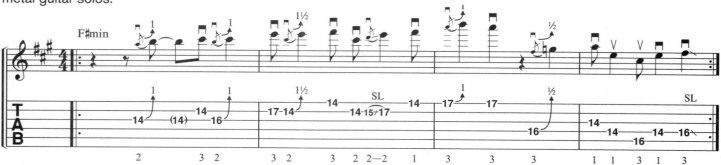

Licks for Shape 2

This Shape 2 lick is a legato run. Make sure your pull-offs sound as loud as the picked notes. The accents are interesting in this one; the 16th notes in each bar are divided into groups of 2, 4, 2, 4, and 4 in descending patterns.

This lick is also based around Shape 2 and uses a few legato rhythms in short bursts. The main theme stated in bar 1 repeats in bar 3. The lick finishes with a wide vibrato.

Licks for Shape 3

In both classic rock and metal, bending can be used in a quick lead context (think of the "Stairway to Heaven" solo). Here we are going to explore developing that skill in a fun, repetitive loop.

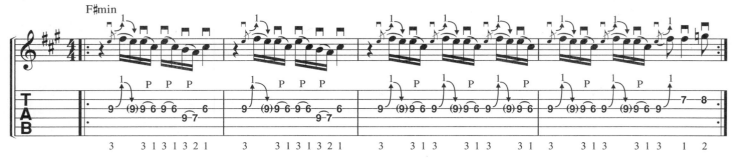

This lick is also in Shape 3 and focuses on alternate-picked 16th notes. They might feel fast, but make sure they are in time and have a comfortable sound.

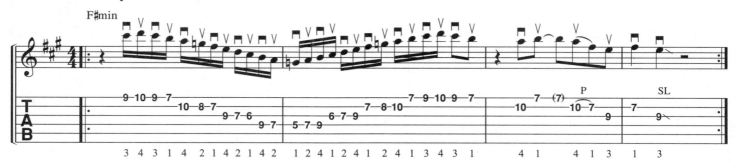

Licks for Shape 4

The first lick for Shape 4 stretches out of the shape a bit. In bars 1 and 3, each note is double picked, and the line outlines what is essentially an expanded power chord. It doesn't get more metal than that!

This lick is develops another key legato phrase with the rolling technique discussed on page 42 (Lick for Shape 1). Legato notes flow on the 4th string while notes on the 3rd string are accented, requiring the fingers to flatten out for a split second to cover them.

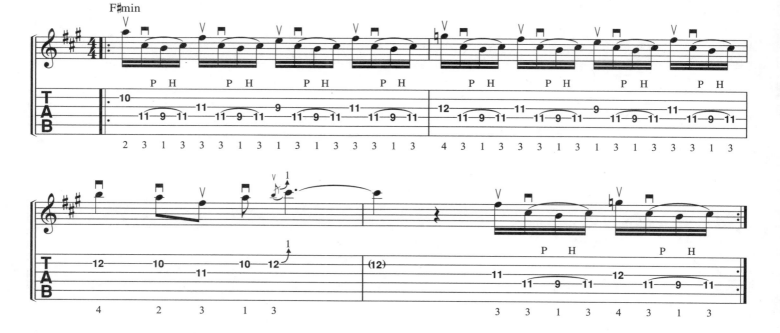

Licks for Shape 5

This Shape 5 lick begins sparse and becomes much more dense at the end. For the 16th-note phrase at the end, use economy picking exclusively, but feel free to experiment with playing it with alternate picking.

F# Minor Blues
Shape 5

11 12 13 14 15

For this last lick in Shape 5, there is a quick sweep-picked phrase that incorporates an arpeggio across all six strings. Metal guitarists often learn sweep arpeggios but have a difficult time making them fit the context of a solo or melody. They can sound contrived and just thrown in for no real reason.

Sweeping and arpeggio playing are helpful for going from very high notes to low notes quickly. Notice that the sweep arpeggio here also includes hammer-ons and pull-offs for a smooth, legato sound.

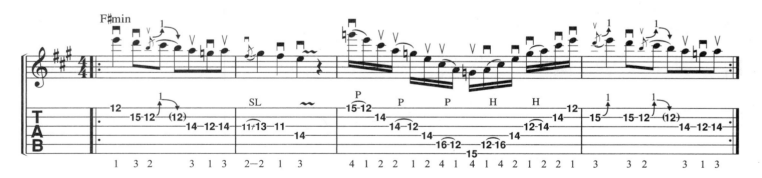

THE GRAND RYMAN PEWS
(Country Rock in G)

Track 12 (Full Mix)
Track 12A (Minus Guitar Lead)

Roadmap

Eight total choruses: head, keyboard solo, guitar solo, keyboard solo, guitar solo, keyboard solo, guitar solo, head.

Overview

The Ryman Theater, one of the most historic venues in America, was home to the Grand Ole Opry from 1943–1974. It was first built as a church, and when it was converted into a theater the wooden pews were kept. The acoustics are said to be among of the best in the world. Located off Broadway in Nashville, Tennessee, this theater has showcased all of the greatest early country stars, including legends like Hank Williams, Patsy Cline, and Johnny Cash.

This song pays respect to that great Nashville tradition with the first riff featuring hybrid picking throughout. Also, take note of how the bends in this tune imitate a pedal steel.

- General form: I–I–IV–IV–V–V–I–I
- Key: G Major
- ♩ = 150 BPM

Listening Suggestions

Joe Maphis: "Flying Fingers"
Joe Maphis is the link between blazing bluegrass virtuosity and electric country guitar. He overdubbed lead lines in octaves in the studio and played a doubleneck guitar with a lower- and higher-octave neck on stage.

Albert Lee: "Fun Ranch Boogie"
Albert Lee first released the song "Country Boy," in which sang and played lead guitar, in 1971. It gave the world its first glimpse into his incredible technique and feel. Since then, Lee has established himself as one of the most influential guitarists in country music.

Soloing

When soloing over this tune, it's important to accommodate the chord changes in your lead lines. For the G Major chord (I), use the G Major scale or the G Minor Blues scale; for the C (IV), use C Major Blues; and for the D (V), use the D Major Blues scale. The song is in the key of G, so you could just play the G Major scale, but it really helps to outline each chord. Also, chromaticism is welcome, so try to fill leaps with chromatic passing tones. Since this song is in the key of G, any and all of your open strings can be used in the context of your solo. The licks in this chapter are in closed positions so that they can easily be transposed, but take time to check out how incorporating open strings can add to your lead lines.

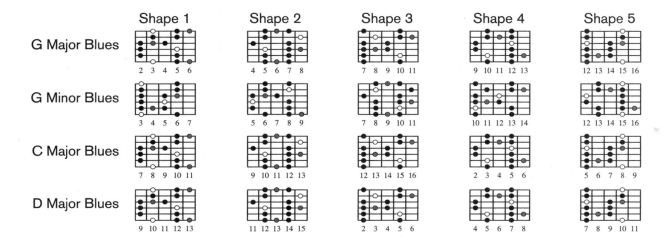

Licks

Lick for Shape 1

Bar 2 of this lick emphasizes the F♯ leading tone, which works well for the V chord (D). Try moving this idea to focus on the 3rd of each chord: the B of G Major (I); the E of C Major (IV); and the F♯ of D Major (V).

G Major Blues
Shape 1

Lick for Shape 2

There are several bends in this lick: both whole-step and subtle quarter-step bends to give extra weight to certain notes. Even at this fast pace, make sure your eighth notes are perfectly in the pocket.

G Major Blues
Shape 2

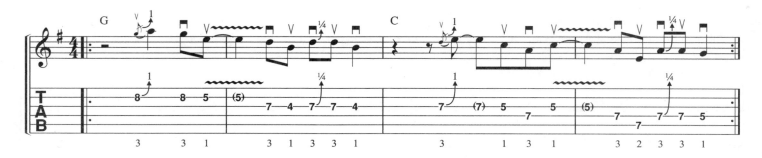

Lick for Shape 3

This lick features a fast run that you can dress up with hybrid picking—using percussive fingerpicking with both the middle and ring fingers. Remember to make sure your hammer-ons and pull-offs match the volume of your picked notes.

G Major Blues
Shape 3

Lick for Shape 4

This lick for Shape 4 uses the full seven-note G Major scale. Using economy picking here will make switching between leaps and adjacent notes a bit easier. But, feel free to try it with strict alternate picking if you prefer. Because the lick is a steady stream of 16th notes, practice looping it with a metronome to help make it feel natural.

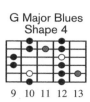

G Major Blues
Shape 4

9 10 11 12 13

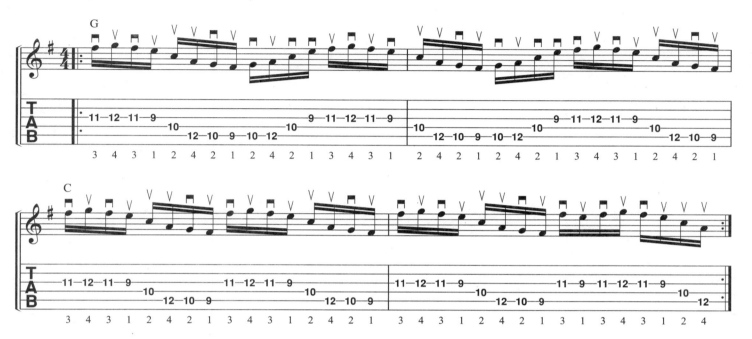

Lick for Shape 5

This last lick is for Shape 5 and features a few new notes. You can transpose this lick, and any of the licks in this chapter, by simply moving it up five frets (or down seven frets) for the IV chord (C) and up seven frets (or down five) for the V chord (D). If the notes are simply the major blues scale, then it works. If the notes step a bit outside, they may need some slight adjusting.

G Major Blues
Shape 5

12 13 14 15 16

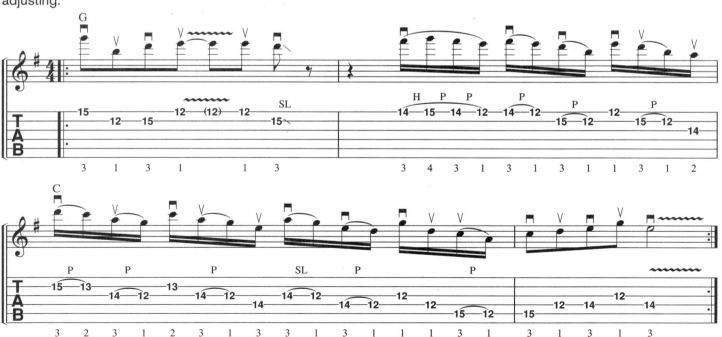

SOMETIMES LESS IS FILLMORE
(Rock Blues in G# Minor)

Track 13 (Full Mix)
Track 13A (Minus Guitar Lead)

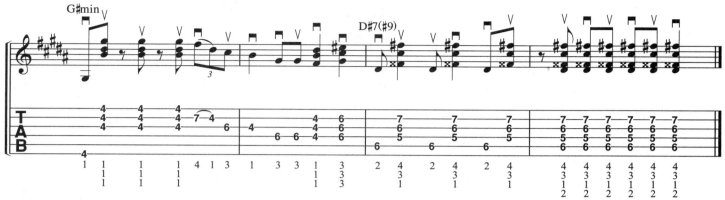

Roadmap

Six total choruses: head, guitar solo (two choruses), keyboard solo, guitar solo, head.

Overview

The Fillmore West, located in San Francisco, CA, and the Fillmore East in New York City, are two legendary establishments of culture and musical art. Both clubs were an essential part of the 1960s and '70s rock movement, hosting artists like Jefferson Airplane, Grateful Dead, Big Brother and the Holding Company, The Allman Brothers Band, Santana, Neil Young, Derek and the Dominoes, and Miles Davis.

This song is focused on putting that sound and vibe under your fingers. During the '60s and '70s, there was a blues revival that had a strong impact on guitarists like Jimi Hendrix, Eric Clapton, Carlos Santana, Jimmy Page, and Mike Bloomfield. They continued the tradition of blues greats like Muddy Waters, Freddie King, and John Lee Hooker. "Sometimes Less Is Fillmore" is a fast minor blues in a swing feel. It is played quickly, so even though the chart is 24 bars long, it is really just a 12-bar blues form. Don't forget to swing the eighth notes.

- General form: i | i | i | i | i | i | i | i | i | iv | iv | iv | iv | i | i | i | i | v | v | iv | iv | i | i | V | V
- Key: G♯ Minor
- ♩ = 150 BPM, Swing 8ths

Listening Suggestions

Jimi Hendrix: "Hear My Train a Comin'"
Jimi Hendrix is such an icon and important voice in guitar and rock culture that any of his songs could be a source of inspiration. Even if you've heard this song before, check it out again.

Santana: "Black Magic Woman"
This is one of the most famous minor blues jams of the 1960s. Carlos Santana's tone and leadership on this song established a Latin blues-rock anthem.

The Allman Brothers Band: "Statesboro Blues"
Duane Allman accomplished more in his short life than most guitar players who lived three times as long. His presence on stage and in the studio was immense. This song is one of his best known. To get a better feel for his style, please feel free to try some of the licks in this chapter with a slide.

Soloing

There are several options when it comes to soloing on a minor blues in G♯. You can, of course, just jam on a G♯ Minor Blues scale, but it will sound more impressive if you make the changes. A good approach is to play a G♯ Minor Blues or G♯ Harmonic Minor for the G♯min (i) chord; C♯ Minor Blues for the C♯min (iv) chord; and D♯ Minor Blues for the D♯min (v) chord. The last V7 chord (D♯7♯9) found in the last two bars is a dominant chord, so you could use a D♯ Dominant ♭9 Pentatonic scale or D♯ Phrygian Dominant (the fifth mode of G♯ Harmonic Minor).

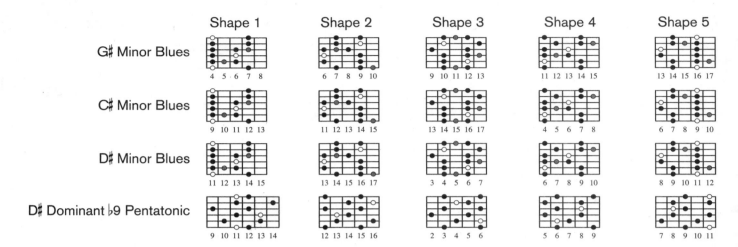

Lick for Shape 1

This lick is all about the slow bend. Be exact with the rhythms to get into the pocket, and be sure to swing the eighths. The bend begins right before beat 1 of bar 2 and takes its time to arrive to its full peak—where it hits the root note G♯. Finally, the lick concludes with a descending pull-off figure.

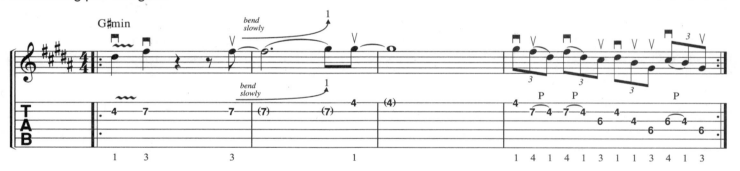

Lick for Shape 2

This lick starts out with pull-off licks that feature wide leaps to give the beginning of this melodic phrase a unique sound. In contrast, the rest of the lick uses really simple, long rhythms.

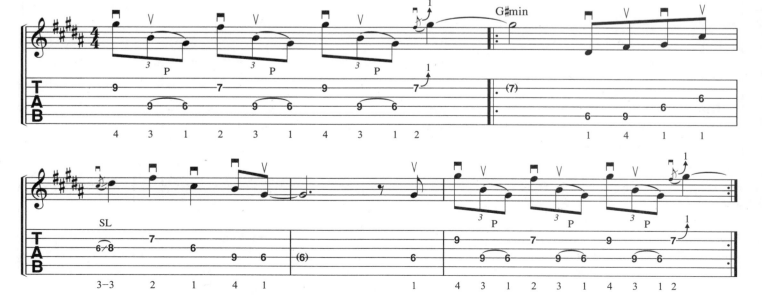

Lick for Shape 3

Here is another example of rhythmic superimposition. This time, triplets are phrased in two-note groups. This lick also uses the pedal-point concept we learned about on page 18, Licks for Shape 3. Using a pedal point can sometimes give you a Classical sound, but here it has more of a blues harmonica effect.

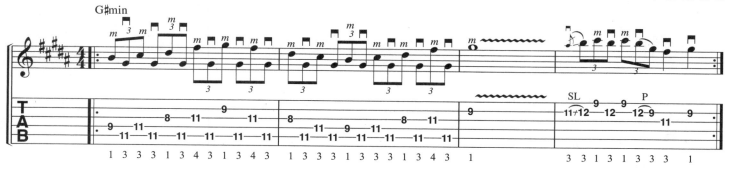

Lick for Shape 4

This is a basic triplet legato lick that moves through the scale to form triadic sounds. It is a great way to develop and build a solo. Work on the fingering until you can explore this idea all over the neck and in different keys.

Lick for Shape 5

Here is another blues phrasing idea to work on. Repeat the rhythm: quarter–eighth, quarter–eighth, etc. You can repeat this idea as much as you like, but in this lick it breaks away with a quick hammer-on/pull-off idea and a descending phrase that leaps in 4ths.

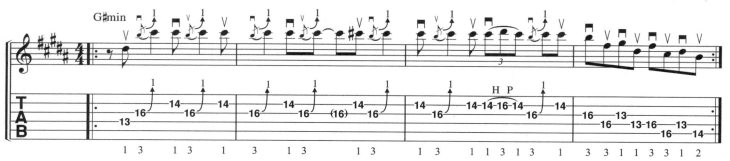

To Be or to CBG Be?

(Alternative Rock in A)

Track 14 (Full Mix)
Track 14A (Minus Guitar Lead)

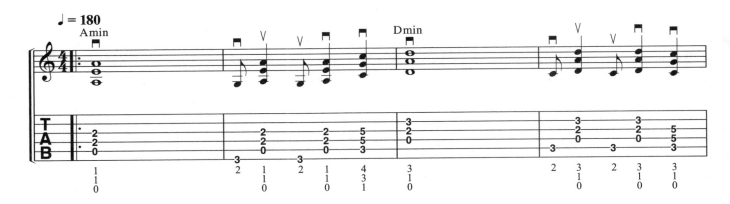

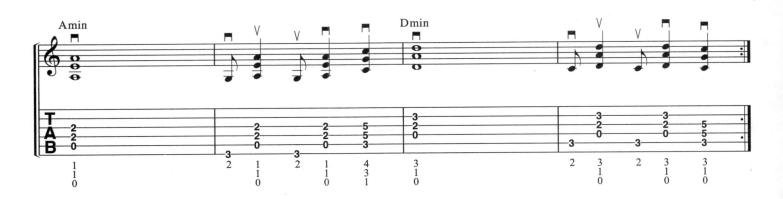

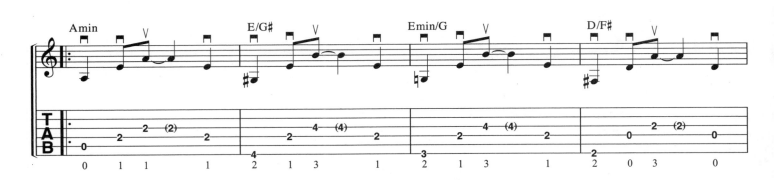

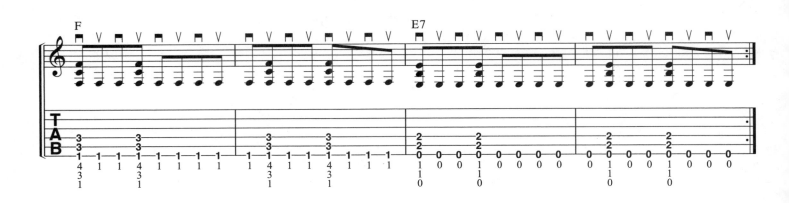

Roadmap

Six total choruses: head, guitar solo, keyboard solo, guitar solo, keyboard solo, head.

Overview

The club CBGB was at the heart of New York City rock and roll for many years. The careers of artists like The Ramones, Patti Smith, Television, Talking Heads, Misfits, Blondie, and The Police were launched there. Even though CBGB stood for "Country, Blue Grass, and Blues," the venue at 315 Bowery St. mostly hosted rock, punk, post-punk, and the cutting-edge sounds on the day.

"To Be or to CBG Be" chugs away in this vein, starting with riffs based on power chords that alternate between A and D. The second section does a walk down through a descending chord progression and ends up on the V chord (E7) to build up tension and to bring it back to the top.

- General form: i | i | iv | iv | i | i | iv | iv, Bridge: i | V | v | IV | ♭VI | ♭VI | V | V
- Key: A Minor
- ♩ = 180

Listening Suggestions

The Ramones: "Rock & Roll High School"
This is an iconic song from the group that largely defined the New York punk-pop sound. Guitarist Johnny Ramone threw down heavy power chords and riffs.

Television: "Marquee Moon"
The band Television was an integral part of the 1970s New York rock scene. They recorded in a raw, stripped down manner but drew from jazz and improvisational influences. This song is the title track from their influential debut album. Guitarists Tom Verlaine and Richard Lloyd played dueling guitar parts, often in a unique angular style.

Soloing

While you could solo over this tune entirely with the A Minor Blues scale, there are other options for making the changes.

The first section is simply A Minor to D Minor, so use the A Minor Blues scale for the A Minor chord and the D Minor Blues scale for the D Minor chord. When we move to the bridge section, the A Minor Blues scale can work but it may miss the intricacies of the progression. The bass line for the chord progression forms the descending melody of A–G♯–G–F♯–F–E. First and foremost with soloing, try to think in terms of arpeggios for these chords. You can use A Natural Minor or A Minor Blues scales for A Minor but you'll need to make alterations for the other chords. For E/G♯, you could play E Phrygian Dominant (A Harmonic Minor from the fifth degree) or E Dominant ♭9 Pentatonic. For the Emin/G chord, you can play an E Minor Blues scale or go back to A Natural Minor. For the D/F♯ chord, you can play A Dorian (D Mixolydian), D Major Blues, or D Dominant 9 Pentatonic. For the F Major chord, you could use A Natural Minor (F Lydian) or F Major Blues. For the last chord, E Major, either E Phrygian Dominant (A Harmonic Minor) or E Dominant ♭9 Pentatonic would work. Please refer to the appendix on page 78 for the scale shapes used throughout.

Lick for Shape 1

This lick will give you some interesting ideas for soloing with the A Minor Blues scale. Even though you should be familiar with this scale shape, there are always new ways to approach it. This legato phrase provides a new rhythmic approach that you can use to help generate ideas.

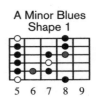

A Minor Blues
Shape 1

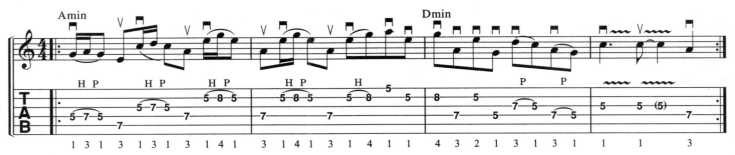

Lick for Shape 2

This legato lick with hammer-ons and pull-offs will help you get into the groove of steady triplets. The last two measures provide space, in contrast to the first two measures which are filled with notes.

A Minor Blues
Shape 2

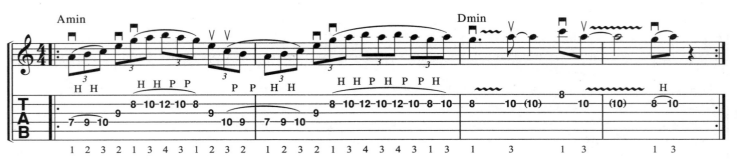

Lick for Shape 3

Let's look at a funky way to play legato licks in a fast, straight groove. Once you get this idea down, try applying it to the chord progression. The third measure contains a chromatic legato lick that uses all four left-hand fingers. The lick ends on the 9th of the scale.

A Minor Blues
Shape 3

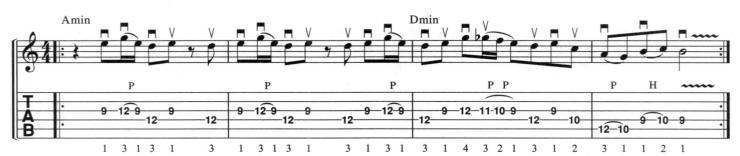

Lick for Shape 4

This lick starts with an arpeggio leading up to a bend. Then, the lick explores rhythmic phrasing that creates a three-beat superimposition (three eighth notes–eighth rest–quarter rest) over four-beat measures.

A Minor Blues
Shape 4

12 13 14 15 16

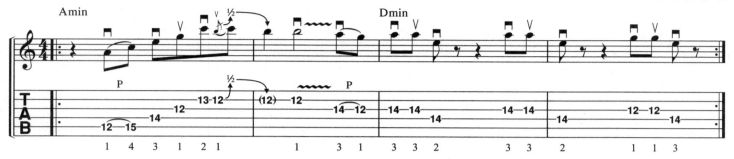

Lick for Shape 5

The steady eighth notes in this lick may not be that interesting, but the melodic contour makes up for that. This lick mixes leaps with stepwise motion that often switch directions. End the lick with a heavy vibrato that matches the groove of the tempo.

A Minor Blues
Shape 5

14 15 16 17 18

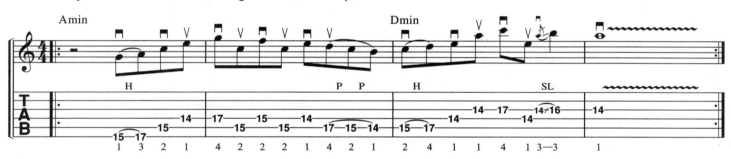

HEAVY AS ROX
(Heavy Metal in D)

Track 15 (Full Mix)
Track 15A (Minus Guitar Lead)

⑥ = D ♩ = 200

Roadmap

Riff A (four times), riff B (one time), riff C (four times), riff A (four times), riff B (two times), riff D (10 times), riff E (four times), riff A (four times), riff B (one time), riff C (four times), riff A (four times), riff B (four times).

Overview

This song is named after the legendary Hollywood, CA club The Roxy. While the list of bands that have played there is impressive, what is perhaps more impressive is the discography of live recordings from this venue, including albums by Bob Marley, Frank Zappa, Bruce Springsteen, NOFX, Social Distortion, and more. The Roxy books touring acts of all genres of music but is most known for playing an integral part in promoting hard rock and heavy metal music, and this song is a tribute to that sound.

This song uses Drop D tuning, where the low E string is tuned down to D, and also features five very different riffs. Have fun, and play with attitude.

- General form: A section: i | i | ♭VI | ♭VII, B section: i | ♭IV | ♭III | ♭VII iv
- Key: D Minor
- ♩ = 200

Listening Suggestions

Pantera: "War"
Pantera guitarist Dimebag Darrell helped metal progress into the intense, heavy grooving genre we know today. His lead and rhythm guitar chops have influenced an entire generation of metal shredders.

Slayer: "Raining Blood"
Slayer was formed in the early 1980s by guitarists Jeff Hanneman and Kerry King. Their extreme and unpredictable style showcased chromatic riffs that don't necessarily fit into a specific scale. Visually and lyrically, their tracks are dark and helped pioneer the sound of thrash metal.

Soloing

Metal is predominantly about rhythm chops, but when it is time to solo, there aren't as many harmonic boundaries as with other styles of music. You can go totally out and not solo in any key at all and it can work, but proceed with caution, of course. Also, the rule of "if the band plays slow, solo fast; if the band plays fast, solo slow" doesn't necessarily apply here. Generally, when the lead break comes over fast riffs, metal guitarists will just rip into it as well. As always, taste is key. Gaining experience playing chromatically, with exotic scales, or out of key will enable you to branch out with new, exciting sounds. Some of the scale shapes are shown in standard tuning, so if you are in Drop D don't use the thickest string or transpose those notes.

Many metal guitarists, such as Dimebag Darrell, will make extensive use of the minor blues scale, modes (such as Aeolian, Phrygian, Locrian, etc.), and arpeggios. Experiment with various techniques, such as legato, different types of picking (sweep, alternate, economy, tremolo), harmonics, and, if you have one, whammy-bar tricks.

Licks

D Minor Blues
Shape 1

10 11 12 13 14

Lick for Shape 1

This lick is an example of incorporating notes from outside of your main scale. You will notice there are a few notes in this lick that are outside of the D Minor Blues scale. For example, the E note in the first measure comes from the natural minor scale.

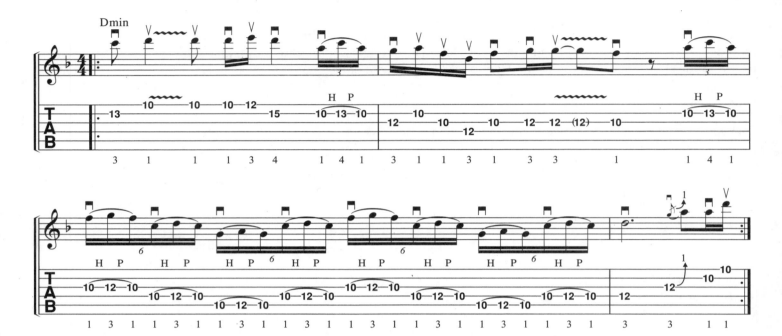

D Minor Blues
Shape 2

12 13 14 15 16

Lick for Shape 2

This lick explores the second shape of the blues scale and uses a few natural minor notes as well. It begins with a bending lick and then ventures into faster picking rhythms.

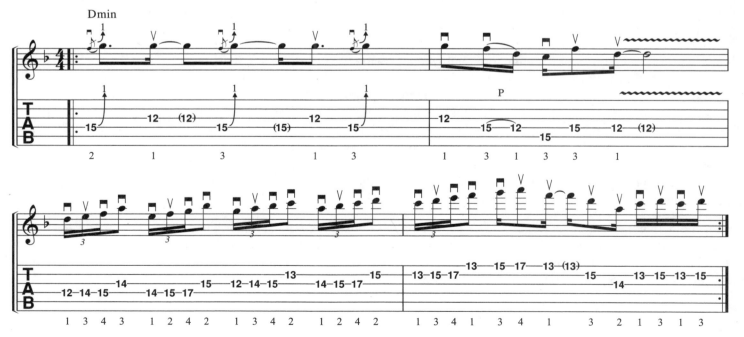

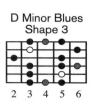

Lick for Shape 3

This lick starts with a left-hand dampened hit on the downbeat to set up a syncopated lick that directly follows. The phrase ends with a legato pattern that jumps down the string sets.

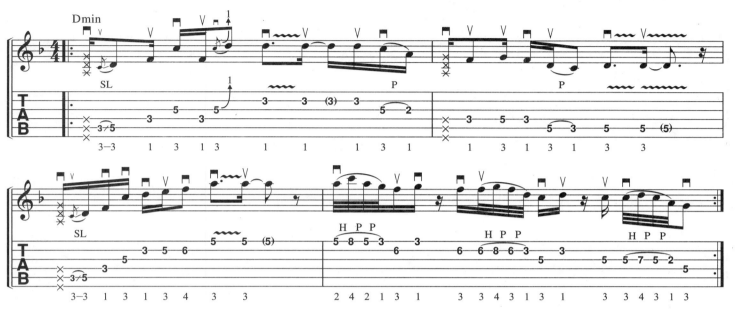

Lick for Shape 4

This lick works well to build up the tension in a metal groove. It starts out with two notes played with heavy vibrato. Then it moves to a faster phrase that includes a few leaps, and it finally ends with a unison bending lick to build up intensity.

Lick for Shape 5

This lick for Shape 5 works on octave-bending ideas. Here you are play a note, then bend up from a whole step below the octave of that note. The wide reaches of this phrase will really give your solo a distinct sound.

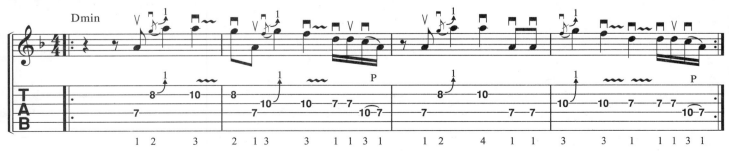

VULCAN ARMADILLO

(Country Rock in C)

Track 16 (Full Mix)
Track 16A (Minus Guitar Lead)

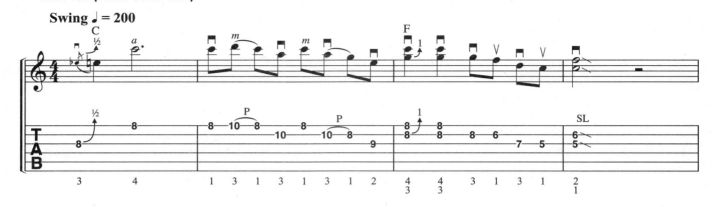

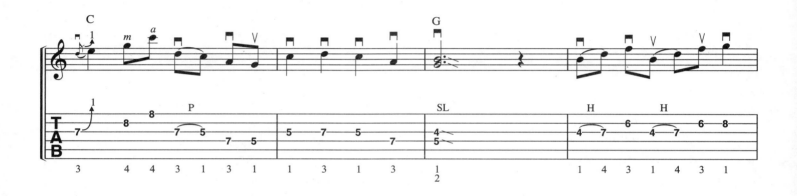

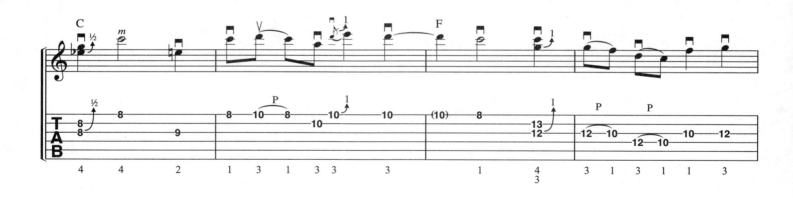

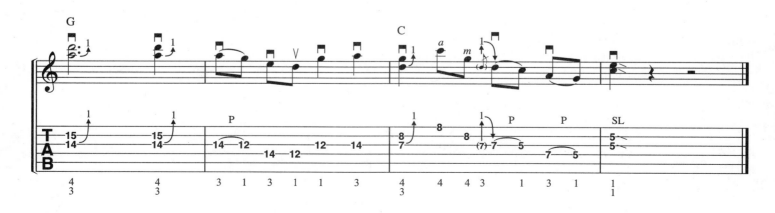

Roadmap

11 total choruses: head, guitar solo, keyboard solo, guitar solo, keyboard solo, guitar solo, keyboard solo, guitar solo, keyboard solo, guitar solo, head.

Overview

This song's inspiration is a now-closed venue called Armadillo World Headquarters in Austin, TX. This club's predecessor was a venue called the Vulcan Gas Company. Thus, "Vulcan Armadillo" serves as a tribute to the two venues that occupied that space. In the 1970s, the Armadillo World Headquarters was like the Fillmore of Austin. It featured many top acts, including Willie Nelson, Ray Charles, Stevie Ray Vaughan, ZZ Top, Freddie King, Frank Zappa, Bruce Springsteen, and even AC/DC, who played their first American show there.

This song is inspired by Austin country and blues. It's a fast country swing song with plenty of hybrid picking, pedal steel-emulating bends, fast bluegrass-type passages, and lots of bluesy soloing. When you play this fast swing feel, practice with a metronome to solidify your rhythm. Eventually, this will become second nature. Now jump on in and have fun!

- General form: I | I | IV | IV | I | I | V | V | I | I | IV | IV | V | V | I | I
- Key: C Major
- ♩ = 200 Swing 8ths

Listening Suggestions

Jimmy Bryant: "Sugar Foot Rag"
Jimmy Bryant is known as one of the fastest guitar pickers in country music history. He used to have a duo with the great pedal steel guitarist, Speedy West.

Steve Morse: "John Deere Letter"
Guitarist Steve Morse developed a signature sound that fuses country influences with rock. From his pop days as a guitarist in Kansas to his fusion music with the Dixie Dregs and his solo work playing on the G3 tour with Joe Satriani and Steve Vai, Morse has been a huge influence on guitarists of many styes, but particularly country rock.

Johnny Hiland: "Barnyard Breakdown"
Johnny Hiland has been one of the most sought-after guitarists in the Nashville, TN music scene. His recording credits include artists like Hank Williams III, Toby Keith, and Randy Travis.

Soloing

This song has a really fast swing feel, so soloing will require a different approach than for a tune in a straight feel. Practice your scales, legato playing, and picking technique for fast swing eighth notes to get familiar with the feel. Another thing to get used to is how the band plays in this feel. The snare drum is traditionally played fast here, so listen to the snare to lock in while you play rhythm guitar and also while you solo.

The other thing to be aware of is the harmony. The chord progression is very precise on this tune, so accenting the I, IV, and V chords as you solo is essential. For the C chord (I), you can play C Major Blues, C Minor Blues (occasionally), or the C Major scale. For the F chord (IV), you can play the F Major Blues scale or just the C Major scale focused on the notes of the F scale. For the G chord (V), you can play the G Major Blues scale or just the C Major scale focused on the G notes. Chromatic lines work well in general, and you can target the notes of each chord with *approach tones* (one or several chromatic notes stepping up or down before they resolve on chord tones).

Licks

Lick for Shape 1

This first lick will help you get into a swing feel at a fast tempo. Notice there are chromatic notes that blend the major blues scale with the major scale.

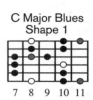

C Major Blues
Shape 1

7   8   9   10   11

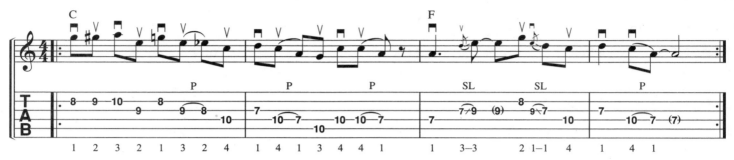

Licks for Shape 2

Here is another lick to get you into the vibe and phrasing of the fast swing feel. The arpeggio in the first bar should be sweep-picked using all downstrokes. The timing here is crucial, so make sure to pay close attention to it.

C Major Blues
Shape 2

9   10   11   12   13

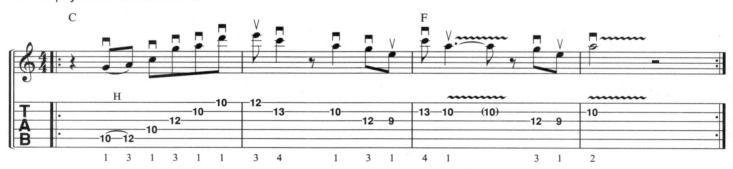

Here's another lick with Shape 2. This one uses the rolling technique; flatten your 3rd and 1st fingers at the points where you cross strings.

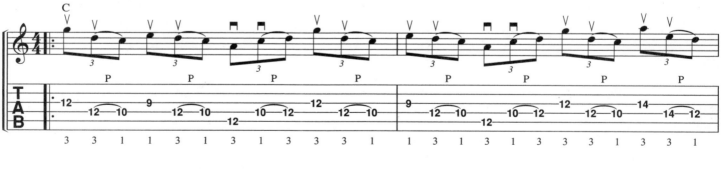

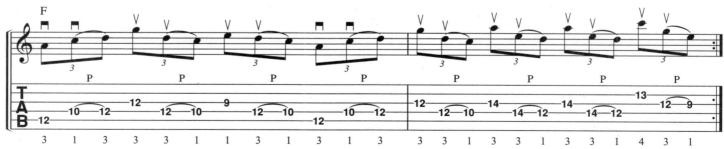

Lick for Shape 3

With this lick, quarter notes are combined with dotted quarter notes. It works great over the I chord (C), but you can transpose it for the IV chord (F) by moving it up five frets (or down seven) and adapt it for the V chord (G) by going up seven frets (or down five).

C Major Blues
Shape 3

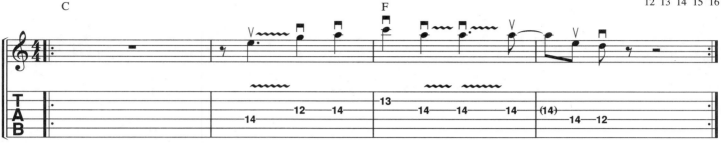

Licks for Shape 4

This is another eighth-note lick that will give you some ideas for phrasing. It includes notes from outside the major scale to add color to the lick.

C Major Blues
Shape 4

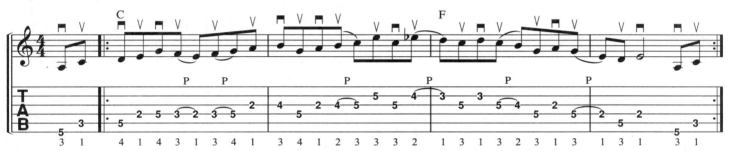

This lick for Shape 4 uses the rolling technique as it moves across string sets. The end of the lick features a slide into the 5th fret and a pull-off through chromatic notes.

Lick for Shape 5

There are two contrasting sections in this lick for Shape 5. The first is a sparse phrase with plenty of vibrato. The second part uses a hammer-on pattern that combines stepwise scalar motion with leaps.

C Major Blues
Shape 5

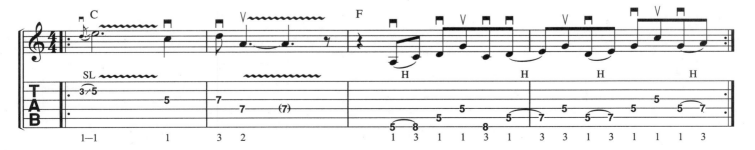

SCALE APPENDIX

Major Scale: 1–2–3–4–5–6–7–8

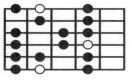
Shape 1

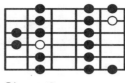
Shape 2

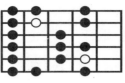
Shape 3

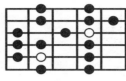
Shape 4

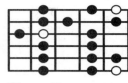
Shape 5

Aeolian (Natural Minor Scale): 1–2–♭3–4–5–♭6–♭7–8

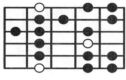
Shape 1

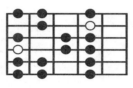
Shape 2

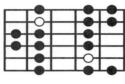
Shape 3

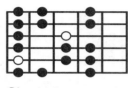
Shape 4

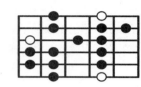
Shape 5

Major Pentatonic Scale: 1–2–3–5–6–8

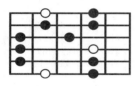
Shape 1

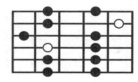
Shape 2

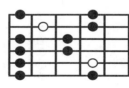
Shape 3

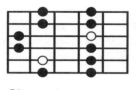
Shape 4

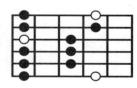
Shape 5

Minor Pentatonic Scale: 1–2–♭3–4–5–♭7–8

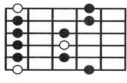
Shape 1

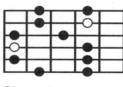
Shape 2

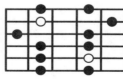
Shape 3

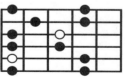
Shape 4

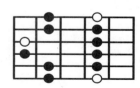
Shape 5

Major Blues Scale: 1–2–♭3–3–5–6–8

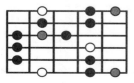
Shape 1

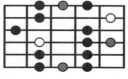
Shape 2

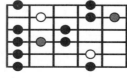
Shape 3

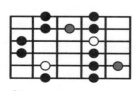
Shape 4

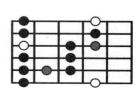
Shape 5

Minor Blues Scale: 1–♭3–4–♭5–5–♭7–8

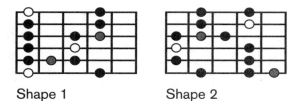 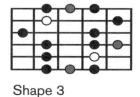 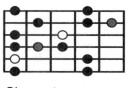 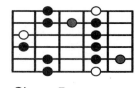

Shape 1   Shape 2   Shape 3   Shape 4   Shape 5

Lydian: 1–2–3–♯4–5–6–7–8

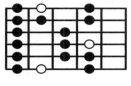 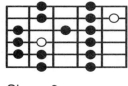 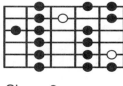 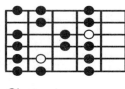 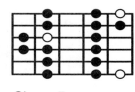

Shape 1   Shape 2   Shape 3   Shape 4   Shape 5

Mixolydian: 1–2–3–4–5–6–♭7–8

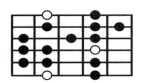 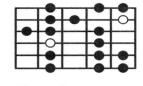 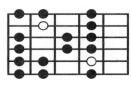 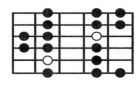 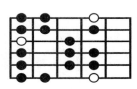

Shape 1   Shape 2   Shape 3   Shape 4   Shape 5

Dorian: 1–2–♭3–4–5–6–♭7–8

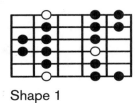 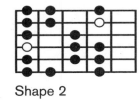 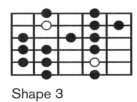 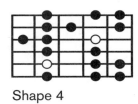 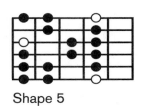

Shape 1   Shape 2   Shape 3   Shape 4   Shape 5

Phrygian: 1–♭2–♭3–4–5–♭6–♭7–8

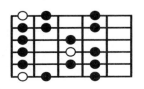 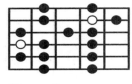  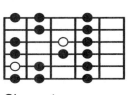 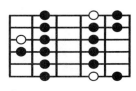

Shape 1   Shape 2   Shape 3   Shape 4   Shape 5

Harmonic Minor: 1–2–♭3–4–5–♭6–7–8

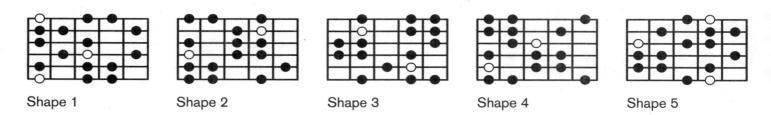

Shape 1   Shape 2   Shape 3   Shape 4   Shape 5

Phrygian Dominant: 1–♭2–3–4–5–♭6–♭7–8

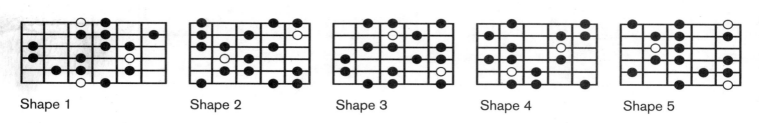

Shape 1   Shape 2   Shape 3   Shape 4   Shape 5

Dominant 9 Pentatonic: 1–2–3–5–♭7–8

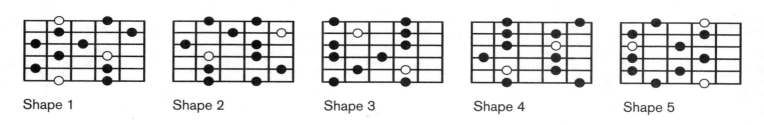

Shape 1   Shape 2   Shape 3   Shape 4   Shape 5

Dominant ♭9 Pentatonic: 1–♭2–3–5–♭7–8

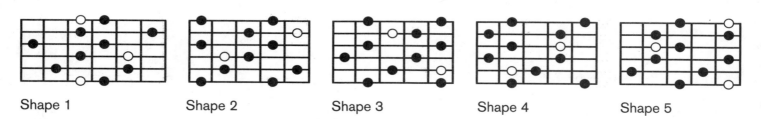

Shape 1   Shape 2   Shape 3   Shape 4   Shape 5